Birds
of Kruger
National Park

Keith Barnes
Ken Behrens

PRINCETON
press.princeton.edu

Published by Princeton University Press,
41 William Street, Princeton, New Jersey 08540
In the United Kingdom: Princeton University Press, 6 Oxford Street,
Woodstock, Oxfordshire OX20 1TR
nathist.press.princeton.edu

First published 2017

British Library Cataloging-in-Publication Data is available

Library of Congress Control Number 2017933359
ISBN 978-0-691-16126-6

Production and design by **WILD**Guides Ltd., Old Basing, Hampshire UK.
Printed in China

10 9 8 7 6 5 4 3 2 1

Keith
This book is dedicated to my parents, who instilled a
passion for nature in a young man, and my wife and
son, for putting up with it in an older one.

Ken
For my parents. Family trips to Yellowstone National
Park, America's equivalent of Kruger, helped to inspire
my love for nature early in life.

Contents

The region

'Kruger' is one of the world's best known national parks, whose mention immediately conjures up visions of an untouched, vast landscape filled with African megafauna and other wildlife. From Kruger's splendid elephants to the most insignificant beetles or butterflies, the sheer diversity of life in this stunning setting creates a lasting impression.

At 20,000 km², Kruger National Park's extent is impressive in itself, about the size of Wales and just a little smaller than Belize – but when combined with a number of private concessions and reserves to the west, the wilderness area extends to nearly 22,000 km². This area is known as the Greater Kruger National Park conservation area (see *page 15*).

The Kruger lies south and west of the Gonarezhou National Park in Zimbabwe and Limpopo National Park in Mozambique, collectively known as the Great Limpopo Transfrontier Park, which contributes another 35,000 km² of protected land. If future plans to expand the protected area to include the Banhine and Zinave National Parks in Mozambique come to pass, a vast conservation area of nearly 100,000 km² will have been created. Important conservation issues remain to be resolved, particularly regarding cross-border poaching and the poisoning of vultures, but this is a region of which southern Africa can justly be proud.

AFRICAN JACANA

About this book

Until relatively recently, most people were drawn to Kruger National Park because of the large mammals, and the chance of being able to see all of the 'Big 5' of Lion, Leopard, African Buffalo, African Elephant and 'Rhinoceros' (of which there are actually two species – Black Rhinoceros and White Rhinoceros). Now, of the nearly 1·4 million visitors that come to the park each year, many have a much broader interest in wildlife. The companion to this book, *Animals of Kruger National Park* (see *page 216*), covers all the mammals, reptiles and frogs that you are most likely to encounter on a 1–2 week visit to Kruger or the adjacent reserves. However, many of these animals spend large parts of the day sleeping or resting, and discovering Kruger's remarkable birds can provide a fascinating alternative at such times. Bird watching can become addictive, so consider yourself warned!

Of the 500 or so birds recorded in Kruger, about half are resident species, some are regular migrants and the remainder are rare or irregular. This book covers 259 species and has been designed to help the visitor identify at least 95% of the birds that are likely to be encountered on any given day. Although the majority of the species included in this book are common and widespread, some rarer birds that are highly conspicuous, distinctive or particularly sought-after are also covered. To improve your chances of encountering Kruger's amazing birdlife, details are also provided on where to go to have the best chance of finding those species that are particularly localized.

If you want to know more about all the birds that might occur in the park and/or are interested in telling apart particularly difficult groups of species such as nightjars or cisticolas, suggestions for further reading are provided on *page 216*.

Although the focus of this guide is the birds of the Kruger National Park, it will be just as useful in areas adjacent to the park where there are similar habitats.

BLUE WAXBILL

The seasons and timing your visit

Kruger has two distinct seasons: a hot and wet rainy period from October to March, and a cool and dry period from April to September. But both seasons are good for birding, offering a different suite of species. The best time to visit for mammals is generally between April and September. At this time, many birds, like the mammals, are easy to locate around permanent water sources such as waterholes and rivers. The weather also tends to be sunny, humidity is

low, temperatures are lower, and there is a reduced risk of contracting malaria. It is worth checking exactly when the mid-year South African school holiday break falls, as if you are planning a visit at that time you will need to book well in advance.

By October and November, the rains will have begun and the bush started to thicken. The number and variety of breeding birds peak during this period, and this is considered to be one of the best times to visit for birding. From December to March the temperature and humidity increase dramatically, and summer school holidays in December and January make for an extremely crowded park. This is, however, one of the best times for birds (especially migrants), and green backgrounds and the abundance of waterbirds provide excellent photographic opportunities, so the pros and cons need to be balanced. After the wet season rains, many birds are attracted to temporary pools and flooded grassland.

The habitats

Kruger's complex geology results in many different habitats. Most of the area comprises flat or gently undulating plains at an altitude of 250–400 m, although there are isolated hills (inselbergs or kopjes). The Lebombo Mountains create a series of low hills in the eastern half of the park. To the north of Punda Maria, and in the extreme southwest, granite, sandstone and quartzite outcrops form rugged hills.

Granitic soils dominate the western half of Kruger and there are basaltic soils in the east; a belt of sandy Karoo sediments lies in between. Adding to this geological diversity, the fact that Kruger stretches through three degrees of latitude gives rise to some 35 different deciduous woodland and savannah micro-habitats in 13 major habitat divisions or biomes (see map on *page 14*). The multitude of different habitat types supports almost every savannah bird species of South Africa. In addition, Kruger is drained from west to east by six large rivers, all of which originate along the great South African escarpment to the west of the park. These rivers add a different dynamic, supporting riverine forest that penetrates the drier savannah.

Despite the region's many subtly different habitat types, most birds have general habitat requirements, and are grouped into four broad categories in this book: **rivers and wetlands**, **plains and open woodland**, **broadleaved woodland**, and **forest and riverine thicket**. These habitat types and the distinctive plant species that characterize them are detailed on *pages 10–12*. However, some bird species do not fit neatly into habitat categories because they range widely in flight, or are seen only at night – and are therefore included in three further categories based on behaviour: **birds of prey and vultures**, **birds of the air**, and **night birds**. Each of these three categories is illustrated and explained on *page 13*.

Rivers and wetlands

Kruger's wetlands comprise a variety of man-made impoundments and natural waterholes, and the Crocodile, Sabie, Sand, Olifants, Letaba and Levuvu Rivers and their tributaries. The rivers are flanked by reedbeds that are used by weavers and kingfishers, while shorebirds live along their banks. Still water attracts storks, ducks, jacanas and herons, while the shy finfoot can be found only on running rivers. Waterholes offer abundant muddy shorelines and open water that is sometimes frequented by waterfowl.

Plains and open woodland

Open grassland with scattered trees, such as **Knobthorn** *Senegalia nigrescens*, occurs on basaltic and Karoo soils, particularly in the southeastern parts of the park (e.g. Satara, Lower Sabie and Crocodile Bridge). The vegetation includes many types of grasses, including **Red Grass** *Themeda triandra*, **Digit Grass** *Digitaria eriantha* and **Buffalo Grass** *Megathyrsus maximus*. Grassland specialist birds, such as bustards and pipits, favour these areas. Where thorn trees such as **Umbrella Thorn** *Vachellia tortilis* dominate, locally called thornveld, eremomelas, apalises, batises and other small insectivorous birds occur.

Baobab *Adansonia digitata* is a giant, broad-trunked tree that is frequent in the northern parts of Kruger.

Marula *Sclerocarya birrea* has distinctive fruits that are rich in vitamin C; it is also used to make the famous cream liqueur Amarula.

Broadleaved woodland

Broadleaved woodland covers more than 65% of the park, although it is most extensive in the western half. Dominant plants include **Sickle Bush** *Dichrostachys cinerea*, **Silver Cluster-leaf** *Terminalia sericea* and a variety of **bushwillows** *Combretum* species. The central part of the park is dominated by **Mopane** *Colophospermum mopane*, an abundant and distinctive tree that can be thinly spread across a grassy shrub savannah, but also occurs with **Marula** *Sclerocarya birrea*, bushwillows and fine-leaved thorn trees/shrubs, or in dense, single-species woodland. The drier, rugged northern region is typified by the familiar bulbous **Baobab** *Adansonia digitata*, which is common in the Limpopo River valley. All of Kruger's camps contain broadleaved woodland habitat, and due to artificial irrigation this is often a lusher version than in the surrounding area and can be particularly rich in birds. Doves, cuckoos, kingfishers, hornbills, barbets, woodpeckers and bush-shrikes dominate this habitat type. See *pages 78–163* for birds that are especially conspicuous and common in the park's camps.

Forest and riverine thickets

Whilst large areas of continuous forest are absent in Kruger, there are stands of riparian thicket and forest-like woodland along the banks of the major rivers. Dominant and distinctive plants include **Sycamore Fig** *Ficus sycomorus*, **Fever Tree** *Vachellia xanthophloea*, **Wild Date Palm** *Phoenix reclinata*, **Sausage Tree** *Kigelia africana* and, in the south of the park, **Weeping Boer-bean** *Schotia brachypetala*. Trumpeter Hornbill, Narina Trogon, turacos and some robin-chats favour this habitat type.

YELLOW-BILLED STORKS, AFRICAN OPENBILL AND GREY HERON

Birds of prey and vultures

This is an easily recognised group, and the charismatic nature of birds of prey make them favourites with park visitors. Some are common and conspicuous, while others are elusive and difficult to observe. Birds of prey hunt in a variety of different habitat types and for this reason have been combined into a single category in this book so that similar species can be more easily compared. The diversity and abundance of birds of prey in Kruger makes it one of the best parks in the world for observing this group of birds.

AFRICAN FISH-EAGLE

Birds of the air

Swallows and swifts forage over virtually any habitat, provided there are flying insects to eat and, since they are superficially similar, are covered together in a single category in this book.

SWIFTS

Night birds

Nightjars and owls are the only birds that are likely to be active and seen on a night drive – unless you are lucky enough to bump into a rare courser or perhaps a thick-knee. Since they are most likely to be seen at night, these birds are presented in a separate category, rather than being included in the broad habitat categories in which they typically occur.

BARN OWL

SQUARE-TAILED NIGHTJAR

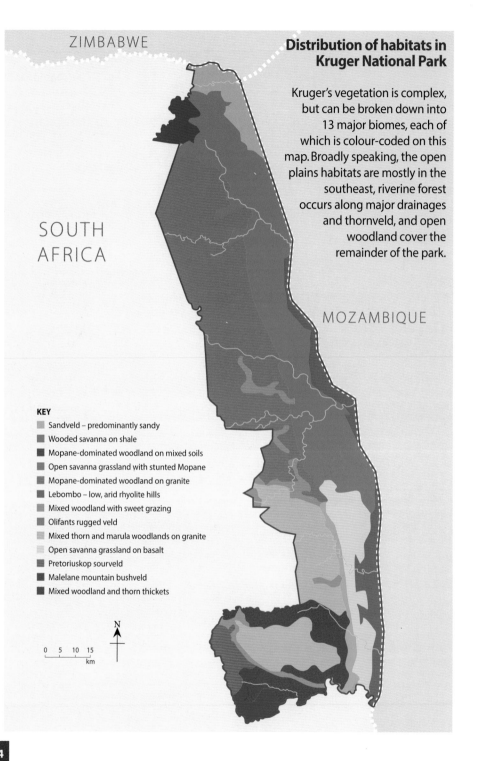

ZIMBABWE

SOUTH
AFRICA

MOZAMBIQUE

Distribution of habitats in Kruger National Park

Kruger's vegetation is complex, but can be broken down into 13 major biomes, each of which is colour-coded on this map. Broadly speaking, the open plains habitats are mostly in the southeast, riverine forest occurs along major drainages and thornveld, and open woodland cover the remainder of the park.

KEY

- Sandveld – predominantly sandy
- Wooded savanna on shale
- Mopane-dominated woodland on mixed soils
- Open savanna grassland with stunted Mopane
- Mopane-dominated woodland on granite
- Lebombo – low, arid rhyolite hills
- Mixed woodland with sweet grazing
- Olifants rugged veld
- Mixed thorn and marula woodlands on granite
- Open savanna grassland on basalt
- Pretoriuskop sourveld
- Malelane mountain bushveld
- Mixed woodland and thorn thickets

N

0   5   10   15
km

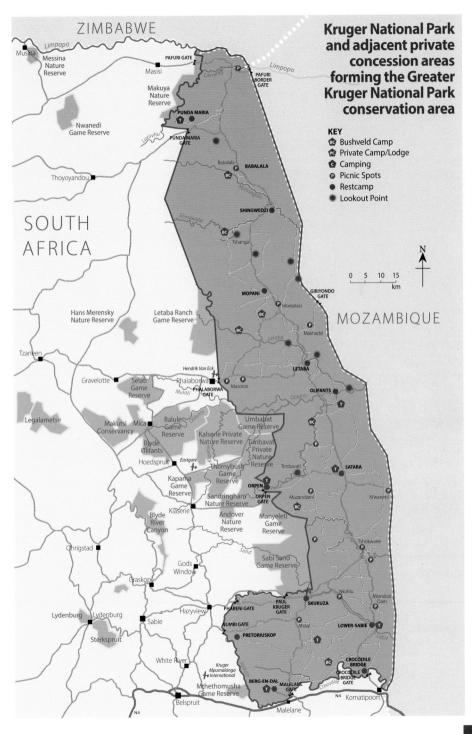

Kruger National Park and adjacent private concession areas forming the Greater Kruger National Park conservation area

KEY
- 🐗 Bushveld Camp
- 🅿 Private Camp/Lodge
- 🏕 Camping
- Ⓟ Picnic Spots
- ● Restcamp
- ✳ Lookout Point

ZIMBABWE

SOUTH AFRICA

MOZAMBIQUE

N

0 5 10 15
km

Musina
Limpopo
Messina Nature Reserve
Masisi
PAFURI GATE
PAFURI BORDER GATE
Limpopo
Luvuvhu
Makuya Nature Reserve
Nwanedi Game Reserve
PUNDA MARIA
Luvuvhu
PUNDA MARIA GATE
Thoyoyandou
Babalala
BABALALA
BC
Shingwedzi
SHINGWEDZI
BC
Tshanga
Mphongolo
MOPANI
Mooiplass
GIRIYONDO GATE
Hans Merensky Nature Reserve
Letaba Ranch Game Reserve
BC
BC
Letaba
Makhadzi
LETABA
Tzaneen
Hendrik Van Eck
Gravelotte
Selati Game Reserve
Phalaborwa
PHALABORWA GATE
Masorini
Mulati
Olifants
OLIFANTS
Legalametse
Makutsi Conservancy
Mica
Balule Game Reserve
Kalserie Private Nature Reserve
Umbabat Game Reserve
BC
Blyde Olifants
Timbavati Private Nature Reserve
Hoedspruit
Eastgate
Thornybush Game Reserve
Timbavati
SATARA
Kapama Game Reserve
Sandringham Nature Reserve
ORPEN
ORPEN GATE
Muzandzeni
N'wanetsi
Blyde River Canyon
Klaserie
Andover Nature Reserve
Manyeleti Game Reserve
BC
Ohrigstad
Tshokwane
Gods Window
Sand
Sabi Sand Game Reserve
Graskop
Nkuhlu
Mlondozi Dam
Lydenburg
Lydenburg
Hazyview
PHABENI GATE
PAUL KRUGER GATE
SKUKUZA
Sabie
NUMBI GATE
Afsaal
LOWER-SABIE
Sterkspruit
PRETORIUSKOP
White River
Kruger Mpumalanga International
CROCODILE BRIDGE
BC
CROCODILE BRIDGE GATE
Mthethomusha Game Reserve
BERG-EN-DAL
MALELANE GATE
Crocodile
N4
Komatipoort
Belspruit
Malelane
N4

15

Introduction to the species accounts

This book covers 259 of the 500 or so species of bird that have been recorded in the Kruger National Park. Six of these species are particularly large and charismatic, and are considered to be the avian equivalent of the traditional 'big 5' mammals – each of these species is designated with a 'Big 6' icon. They are Lappet-faced Vulture (*page 184*), Martial Eagle (*page 188*); Saddle-billed Stork (*page 28*), Kori Bustard (*page 66*), Southern Ground-Hornbill (*page 104*) and Pel's Fishing-Owl (*page 214*).

Kruger is a vital area for many birds of conservation concern, and 21 of the species included in this book are threatened with regional extinction according to *The 2015 Eskom Red Data Book of Birds of South Africa, Lesotho and Swaziland* (Taylor *et al.* 2015, see *page 216*), also known as the Red List. These are highlighted with an icon that indicates their status as Critically Endangered (most precarious) **CR**, Endangered **EN**, Vulnerable **VU** or Near Threatened (least precarious) **NT**.

Most bird books present the species in a strict scientific (taxonomic) order, based on their relationships with one another. However, because this order requires some experience to understand, and is not intuitive to those new to birding, this book

Birds included in this book that are considered regionally threatened		
Hooded Vulture	**CR**	(*page 181*)
White-headed Vulture	**CR**	(*page 185*)
White-backed Vulture	**CR**	(*page 183*)
Yellow-billed Stork	**EN**	(*page 27*)
Saddle-billed Stork	**EN**	(*page 28*)
Southern Ground-Hornbill	**EN**	(*page 104*)
Cape Vulture	**EN**	(*page 182*)
Lappet-faced Vulture	**EN**	(*page 184*)
Tawny Eagle	**EN**	(*page 186*)
Martial Eagle	**EN**	(*page 188*)
Bateleur	**EN**	(*page 191*)
Pel's Fishing-Owl	**EN**	(*page 214*)
African Finfoot	**VU**	(*page 41*)
Secretarybird	**VU**	(*page 180*)
African Crowned Eagle	**VU**	(*page 192*)
Lanner Falcon	**VU**	(*page 194*)
Greater Painted-Snipe	**NT**	(*page 43*)
Abdim's Stork	**NT**	(*page 61*)
Marabou Stork	**NT**	(*page 62*)
Kori Bustard	**NT**	(*page 66*)
European Roller	**NT**	(*page 101*)

Birds included in the 2015 Eskom Red Data Book

categorizes birds according to their favoured habitats or, where more than one habitat-type is used, their dominant behaviour (see *pages 9–13*). In addition, species that look similar are placed alongside one another for ease of comparison, even if they are unrelated.

The common names and species designations used follow the standard reference work *Robert's Birds of Southern Africa* (see *page 216*). However, because the common names for birds differ between reference sources, and often between field guides, and some people may prefer to use scientific names, an alphabetical listing of species by their scientific name is included on *pages 218–220*.

The species accounts vary somewhat in terms of the level of detail provided, but every effort has been made to avoid the use of technical terms and jargon. However, the use of some such terms is inevitable and these are annotated using the images below. For each species, key information includes English name and size (the length (L) of the bird from feet to bill tip, given in cm and inches (")). Birds that spend much time soaring, such as storks, herons, eagles and other birds of prey, are also given a wingspan (WS) measurement to assist in the judgement of relative size in flight. For distinctive looking species, such as Lilac-breasted Roller or Southern Carmine Bee-eater, the photos themselves provide adequate detail for identification, and the text on plumage detail is therefore relatively brief. If an aspect of a species' natural history is particularly interesting, such as its breeding biology, this is covered in the text. Where possible, images of males, females, juveniles and alternative plumages are included and annotated.

Finally, in case you wish to mark off each bird you see, a small check box is placed next to each species name.

Cormorants and darters swim and dive underwater from the surface, to feed on fish, frogs and aquatic insects. Unlike most aquatic birds, they do not have waterproof body feathers, so quickly get cold and waterlogged. As a consequence, they can neither spend too long in the water, nor colonize areas with very low water temperatures. These birds habitually stand on open perches in the sun with outspread wings, both to dry the plumage and to warm the belly to aid digestion. All have short legs, large webbed feet, long wings, rather long tails and kinked necks. Cormorants have thick, hooked bills, while darters have slender, pointed bills.

☐ African Darter
L: 90 cm (35") | WS: 115–128 cm (45–50")

This cormorant-like waterbird is colloquially known as the 'snakebird'. It often swims with its body submerged, so the long, slender neck and slim bill stand up from the water, looking ominously serpentine. It is separated from cormorants by its more elegant shape, small head, slender neck and bayonet-shaped rather than hooked bill. In flight is has a longer tail and a much more slender head and neck than the White-breasted Cormorant. The adult is mostly black, its back adorned with white flecks and streaks. The male has a rufous neck with a white stripe from the eye along the side of the head. Females and juveniles are muted and brown. The African Darter is a common resident and is widespread, preferring placid waters to fast-flowing rivers, and favours areas with dead trees or other platforms where it can perch.

FEMALE

MALE

IMMATURE

☐ White-breasted Cormorant

L: 90 cm (35") | WS: 120–160 cm (47–63")

A bulky, strongly built cormorant with distinctive turquoise eyes. Adult is distinctly pied (blackish with a large white bib), while juvenile is browner and heavily speckled. White-breasted Cormorant is an uncommon resident that breeds in colonies with other waterbirds. Although mostly a fish-eater, it may occasionally eat a neighbour's chick at the breeding colony.

☐ Reed Cormorant

L: 52 cm (20") | WS: 85 cm (33")

A small, long-tailed cormorant. Breeding adult is blackish and has a short black crest above the bill, whereas juvenile is browner overall. It can always be separated from White-breasted Cormorant by its much smaller size, red eyes, and proportionately longer tail. It is a common resident and widespread species.

Herons and egrets stand or stride along the water's edge, waiting patiently for a chance to catch a fish or frog with a lightning strike of the bill.

☐ Goliath Heron
L: 152 cm (60") | WS: 185–230 cm (73–91")

PURPLE HERON

GREY HERON

GOLIATH HERON

This enormous heron with a heavy, dagger-like bill, stands 1·5 m (5 ft) tall. Although superficially similar in coloration to Purple Heron, the Goliath Heron is twice the size, and has a ponderous, laboured flight on long, very broad, rounded wings. The plumage is rufous and grey with a characteristic white throat, and it has a distinctive black bill and legs. Immatures have rustier upperwings than the adult. The Goliath Heron hunts along the large waterways of the Kruger, where it is an uncommon but conspicuous resident. It has a distinct *"kowoork"* barking call that can be heard from up to 2 km (1·2 miles) away. This species is a picky eater, and mainly hunts fish weighing more than 500 g (1·1 lb), stabbing them with open mandibles. Because it takes time to swallow such a large catch, it is vulnerable to the attempts of other birds to pilfer its prey, despite its size. Potential thieves include African Fish-Eagle, Yellow-billed Kite and Saddle-billed Stork.

Purple Heron

L: 85 cm (33") | WS: 120–150 cm

Much smaller and shier than the similarly plumaged Goliath Heron, this relatively slim and delicate heron has a diagnostic black crown, black stripes on the sides of the rufous face, a slim yellow bill, and yellowish rather than black legs. Young birds are almost entirely pale rufous. The Purple Heron is a widespread but uncommon resident, preferring areas with reeds and rushes where it can hide and forage. It is a stalker and prefers to hunt at dawn and dusk from thick cover such as dense reeds, catching fishes, amphibians and insects. When surprised or threatened it will fly or adopt a 'bittern-like' posture, pointing its head skyward, to camouflage itself in the reeds.

Grey Heron L: 97 cm (38") | WS: 155–195 cm (61–77")

This is a large, pale and almost all-grey heron, entirely lacking the rufous hues of the much larger Goliath Heron and more slender Purple Heron. The adult has a distinct black eyebrow that extends behind the head as a fine plume, and a white face, head and foreneck. Juveniles are dingier and greyer on the head. The legs and bill are almost always greenish-yellow. In flight, the underwings are a uniform slate grey, and the upperwings two-toned grey and black. This common resident is frequently encountered on Kruger's freshwater lakes, ponds and impoundments.

GREAT EGRET
NON-BREEDING

LITTLE EGRET
NON-BREEDING

GREAT EGRET
NON-BREEDING

LITTLE EGRET
NON-BREEDING

NB note
gape lines

YELLOW-BILLED
EGRET

☐ Yellow-billed Egret

L: 70 cm (28") | WS: 105–115 cm (41–45")

Similar to Great Egret, this bird is smaller with a less coiled neck, and a relatively shorter bill; the gape line stops beneath the eye instead of extending farther back. The bill is always yellow and the upper half of the leg is often greenish-yellow. An uncommon visitor to Kruger, absent in drier years, it prefers flooded grassland and damp areas that are more widespread during the December to March rains. Although it prefers hunting fishes, frogs and insects, it has been recorded eating nestling bishops (*page 154*).

GREAT EGRET

YELLOW-BILLED
EGRET

LITTLE EGRET

Little Egret L: 64 cm (25") |
WS: 88–106 cm (35–42")

This medium-sized, sleek and elongated white egret has a fine plume on the head, a slender black bill (never yellow) and blackish legs with characteristic bright yellow feet. It is a fairly common and widespread Kruger resident, although numbers may fluctuate depending on local conditions. When feeding, it moves quickly, with agility and dexterity, using its feet to flush aquatic prey in shallow water, and darting about in pursuit. Occasionally it wiggles its yellow toes underwater, either to disturb prey or to lure it closer. In shallow waters it has been known to look for an easy meal by following Hippopotamuses, spoonbills or cormorants that may disturb prey.

Great Egret
L: 92 cm (36") | WS: 131–170 cm (52–67")

Egrets are long-legged, long-necked wading birds, that look like white herons. The largest white egret, the Great Egret, is the size of a Grey Heron (*page 21*). It is similar to the smaller Yellow-billed Egret, but the long neck is often held in a kinked 'S'-shape, and the line of the bill opening (the gape) extends behind the eye – a useful feature at close range. The large dagger-like bill is yellow in non-breeding plumage and black when breeding, when the bird also has a 'cloak' of long, fine, wispy plumes over its back. Its legs are blackish or greenish-yellow above the joint. This is a widespread and common resident of Kruger's dams and rivers.

BREEDING

BREEDING

☐ Green-backed Heron
L: 40 cm (16") | WS: 62–70 cm (24–28")

This very small, compact heron is mostly dark green, with yellow legs, and has a dark cap that can be erected as a short crest. Immatures are browner and streakier than adults. It is a common breeding resident in Kruger. Inconspicuous and solitary, it often stands hunched next to the water, peering downwards, waiting to stab at prey. It has been recorded using bait, such as spiders, insects, bread and even paper, to lure fishes within range. It makes short, quick flights low over the water, with jerky wingbeats, when its pale feet are conspicuous.

☐ Black-crowned Night-Heron
L: 61 cm (24") | WS: 110–120 cm (43–47")

A plump, short-legged, bull-necked heron, active at dawn and dusk. The adult is grey, with a white face, large reddish eyes, and black cap and back. Immatures are brown and streaky, with pale spots on the upperside. An uncommon resident in Kruger, this bird feeds mainly at night, emerging at dusk and often calling a distinctive, odd "*kwoerk*" as it disperses to forage in nearby wetlands. During the day it roosts communally in dense foliage overhanging water, where it can be hard to see. Colonies are the targets of pythons and monitors that will readily prey on unattended chicks.

ADULT

IMMATURE

ADULT

IMMATURE

ADULT

ADULT

☐ Black Heron

L: 51 cm (20") | WS: 90–95 cm (35–37")

The names heron and egret are often interchangeable; this 'heron' is small and slim, more like an all-dark egret, with dark legs and yellow feet. The juvenile is brown and lacks the adult's elongated plumes. Rare and somewhat nomadic in Kruger, it is more frequently recorded between December and March, or in wetter years. It prefers shallow edges of marshes, rivers, dams and lakes. It forages using a unique technique, flinging its wings open and forwards in a stiff arch, and freezing in an 'umbrella' posture for a few seconds. The purpose of this behaviour is unclear, but it may create a patch of shade, so the egret can see more clearly into the water, or it may serve to attract prey, or both.

☐ Squacco Heron

L: 46 cm (18") | WS: 80–92 cm (32–36")

This compact, thick-necked, heron is tan-brown on the head, breast and back, streaked in non-breeding plumage, with all-white wings and tail. At rest, it can be difficult to see, but on taking flight it reveals its startlingly contrasting white wings. When breeding, it has a bluish hue to the face and bill, but at other times the face is yellowish and the head and neck are streaked darker. Squacco Herons tend to be solitary and uncommon but widespread residents in Kruger, preferring water bodies with emergent vegetation where they can skulk inconspicuously.

IMMATURE

ADULT

ADULT

Storks are like large herons with a distinctive long-striding walk and thicker, longer bills. In flight, they have flatter wings and a long, projecting head and neck – unlike herons which retract their head back into the shoulders in flight.

☐ Woolly-necked Stork
L: 86 cm (34") | WS: 150–160 cm (59–63")

A large, erect, dark brown stork, with a greenish and bronze iridescence on the wings and breast, a distinctive ruffed white neck, a white tail, a blackish 'skullcap' and face, and a dark bill with a salmon-pink tip. Although scarce, the Woolly-necked Stork is conspicuous and widespread in Kruger, favouring rivers, pans, dams and other wetlands. The small resident breeding population in Kruger is supplemented by non-breeding visitors from farther north in Africa between November and July. Combined, these number fewer than 300 individuals. It feeds on insects and small vertebrates.

☐ African Openbill
L: 81 cm (32") | WS: 140 cm (55")

This is a medium-sized, all-dark stork with a greenish gloss. The bill is horn-coloured and uniquely concave on the inner cutting edges, creating a diagnostic 6 mm (0·2") gap between the mandibles; at long range the bill appears extended and oval. The slow and laboured flight, and long neck and feet separate it from other dark waterbirds. Uncommon but conspicuous at freshwater wetlands throughout Kruger, it uses its odd bill to extract snails and mussels from their shells, often without breaking them.

A nomadic species, it is an erratic breeder in the park, depending on the condition of the wetlands. The small local population is estimated to fluctuate between 50 and 300 individuals.

EN ☐ Yellow-billed Stork

L: 100 cm (39") | WS: 150–165 cm (59–65")

This is a large, mostly white bird, with black wings, long pinkish-red legs, a distinctive yellow bill and bright red facial skin. In flight it is mostly white with a broad black trailing edge to the underwings, and a distinctive black tail that differentiates it from the grassland-loving White Stork (*page 63*). Young birds are greyish with horn-coloured bills. It is uncommon in Kruger, where the small resident population may be supplemented by non-breeding visitors from farther north in Africa between October and April. It is more tied to wetland habitats than most other storks and forages in muddy pools with its bill partially submerged and open, stirring up prey with its feet, and snapping up fishes and other small creatures upon contact. It is not particularly gregarious, but will congregate when food is abundant.

YELLOW-BILLED STORK

WOOLLY-NECKED STORK

AFRICAN OPENBILL

One of the BIG 6

EN ☐ **Saddle-billed Stork**

L: 142 cm (56") | WS: 240–270 cm (94–106")

This very large, tall, long-legged black-and-white stork has a unique and distinctive bill that is red, yellow and black. The male has dark-brown eyes and frequently a yellow wattle at the bill base, while the female has yellow eyes. In flight, the white belly and underwing pattern – white with a black central line – are diagnostic. The immature looks fluffy and is tan coloured with a dark bill and facial skin. It is a rare but very conspicuous resident bird in Kruger, preferring rivers and large undisturbed wetlands, where it forages for favourites such as catfish, but will also take frogs, birds and insects. Most of South Africa's breeding population occurs in Kruger, which supports around 20–40 pairs, with several stable territories on the Letaba and Levuvu rivers. Large conservation areas such as Kruger are crucial for this species' survival. However, pollution of, and removal of water (for industry and agriculture) from the Letaba, Olifants and Sabie river catchments outside Kruger is reducing the number of Saddle-billed Storks in the park.

The Hamerkop is a prominent species in tribal folklore: Zulus believe it to be a vain bird, ugly yet constantly admiring its reflection in the water; it is also considered a harbinger of death, so to dream about one or have one fly over your house is bad luck.

☐ Hamerkop L: 56 cm (22") | WS: 90–94 cm (35–37")

This dull brown, ibis-type bird has a black bill that is taller than it is wide, and a bushy-crested 'hammer-head', creating an easily recognizable profile. In flight it has distinctive deep wingbeats, and it may occasionally soar very high like a bird of prey, but the long neck separates it from the raptors. Although the Hamerkop is related to storks and pelicans, it is so bizarre that it is placed in its own family. In Kruger it is a common and widespread resident, preferring slow-flowing rivers and dams, adjacent to which it builds its giant (1·5 m | 5 ft wide), roofed, stick nest. These nests are so well built that eagle-owls, Egyptian Geese, raptors and even genets often use them. Hamerkops indulge in unusual rituals, where up to 10 birds gather and run around, making a strange tinny vocalization and fluttering their wings. They have also been recorded 'false mounting' – pretending to mate. Much of this odd behaviour remains unexplained.

IMMATURE

☐ African Spoonbill

L: 91 cm (36") | WS: 120–135 cm (47–53")

A medium-sized, white waterbird with pink-red legs and bare face, and an odd and distinctive flattened, spoon-tipped bill, which is obvious even in flight. African Spoonbill occurs as an irregular visitor to Kruger, where it rarely breeds. It prefers large, quiet, shallow waterbodies and forages by swinging its head from side-to-side as it walks forward in the shallows, slicing its slightly open bill through the water, searching for small fishes and aquatic invertebrates. It may follow Hippopotamuses and Nile Crocodiles to eat creatures disturbed by their movements.

☐ African Sacred Ibis

L: 82 cm (32") | WS: 112–124 cm (44–49")

Ibises are thick-legged, squat, stork-like birds
with characteristic downcurved bills. The
African Sacred Ibis is distinctive, with a white
body, naked black neck and head, and a black
bill. Black plumes on the back often look
like a black feather-duster! The white parts
often become quite soiled when the bird has
been feeding in muddy places. In flight it
has a distinctive shape, and the black head,
neck, legs and trailing edge of the wing give
it a unique pattern. Scarce but widespread
in Kruger, numbers can fluctuate, and at the
driest times it can be absent; it prefers wetland
edges and lush grassland.

☐ Spur-winged Goose L: 85–100 cm (33–39")

A massive, heavily built, long-necked, black goose, with varying amounts of white on the head, belly and wings, and a warty red bill, face and legs. In flight, the white forewings on the black body differentiate it from other waterfowl. The male is much larger than the female. This species is uncommon in Kruger, but can be absent from the park in drier years; numbers often increase after the December to March rains when more wetland habitat becomes available. It forages in a variety of wetland habitats and lush grasslands, feeding mostly on plant matter. It usually nests in vegetation near water but has been known to commandeer the nests of Hamerkop or even Martial Eagle or African Fish-Eagle. The function of the spur on the bend of the wing, which gives the bird its name but is often hidden, is poorly known, but it is used by males in aggressive territorial conflicts.

Little Grebe L: 20 cm (8")

Grebes are swimming birds which dive to feed. They differ from ducks and geese in their narrow, pointed bills and lobed, rather than webbed, toes. Also called the 'Dabchick', the Little Grebe is the smallest species of waterfowl within Kruger. When breeding, it is rufous and dark grey, with a pale spot by the bill, while in non-breeding plumage it is dirty buff with a paler face. Little Grebe numbers fluctuate in Kruger, with it being common during wet periods and absent during droughts. It is widespread on open water bodies, and avoids rivers and fast-flowing water, this bird is often detected by its characteristic trilling call. It nests on floating vegetation on open water, and is rarely seen on land because its legs are set so far back that it is unable to walk far. It rides high on the water with the rear often elevated, sometimes raising its back feathers to expose black skin to the sun to help regulate its body temperature. The Little Grebe dives to catch fishes, tadpoles and insects, and will follow Hippopotamuses to small eat animals they disturb. Like other grebes it will eat its own feathers, which line the digestive tract and prevent injury from small fish bones. It is one of the favoured prey items of the Cape Clawless Otter.

BREEDING

NON-BREEDING

JUVENILE

☐ Egyptian Goose L: 74 cm (29")

A bulky, mostly tan-brown goose with a chestnut back and wings and a distinctive black-tipped, pinkish bill, chestnut eye-ring, and chestnut spot in the centre of the breast. In flight it shows large, eyecatching white ovals on the forewings. It is an abundant resident on wetlands throughout Kruger, usually breeding on ponds or waterholes. Birds frequently give a loud and grating call that draws attention to their presence. A symbol of reverence for the ancient Egyptians, this goose is an excellent parent, capable of driving off crocodiles to protect its young.

☐ White-faced Duck L: 48 cm (19")

This duck often stands upright beside a pond, looking quite long-legged, long-necked and very dark, with a white face. Juveniles are more uniform brown, but still usually show a paler face. It is a common, but highly nomadic, duck in Kruger on still water covered with surface vegetation.

It usually flies in small groups, and frequently calls a characteristic whistling *"wheee-whee-wooo"*, which can sometimes be heard at night. Eats mostly seeds and other plant matter. Numbers increase between December and March when temporary wetlands proliferate, and during wetter years.

☐ Comb Duck L: 56–76 cm (22–30")

A large, odd-looking duck with black wings and white body. Its neck and head are speckled black, and the wings show a greenish iridescence. Males are significantly larger than females, with a grotesque knob-like protuberance on the top of the bill that enlarges during the breeding season. In flight the all-dark wings contrast with the pale body. Young birds are buff below, with dull brown upperparts. The Comb Duck is an uncommon to common resident in Kruger, with numbers increasing between December and March, and during wetter years. It favours freshwater swamps, where it feeds on vegetation by grazing or dabbling. When conditions allow, the males may mate with several females, sometimes forming a harem. Most nests are in tree cavities over water.

MALE

FEMALE

☐ **African Black Duck** L: 56 cm (22")

A chocolate-brown duck with white spots on the back and rump, unmarked underparts, a pale pink-and-black bill and orange legs. In flight it shows a bluish wing panel. The similar Yellow-billed Duck is easily differentiated by its bright yellow bill. African Black Duck is a secretive and scarce resident in Kruger, preferring well-wooded rivers and fast-flowing water, but occasionally visits ponds and dams. Forages mainly at dawn and dusk, when it dabbles for invertebrates and plant matter.

RED-BILLED TEAL

☐ **Red-billed Teal** L: 48 cm (19")

This small, pale duck has a distinctive pink-red bill with a dark saddle, a solid chocolate-brown 'skullcap', and white cheeks. In flight the buff flight feathers with a black stripe stand out on otherwise all-brown wings. Uncommon in wetlands throughout Kruger; numbers increase in December to March, and during wetter years. Prefers open waterbodies and backwaters where seeds and plant matter form the bulk of its diet.

YELLOW-BILLED DUCK

☐ **Yellow-billed Duck** L: 60 cm (24")

A chocolate-brown duck with a vivid yellow bill and white scalloping to the feathers, giving it a scaly appearance, especially on the underparts. In flight it shows a greenish wing panel. The scarce, river-dwelling, African Black Duck is similar, but has plain underparts, a pinkish bill and orange legs. The Yellow-billed Duck is an uncommon resident in Kruger, preferring the southwest between Skukuza and Berg-and-Dal, where it dabbles on freshwater ponds for invertebrates and plant matter.

AFRICAN BLACK DUCK

RED-BILLED TEAL

YELLOW-BILLED DUCK

☐ Common Moorhen L: 30–38 cm (12–15")

A medium-sized and mostly dark rail usually seen at the water's edge. It is readily identified by the large red facial shield and yellow-tipped red bill, yellow-green legs (red above the joint), a characteristic white patch under the tail and white flank stripe. Immatures are all-brown, including the bill, but have the same bold white patches under the tail as adults, and yellow legs. An uncommon and nomadic resident in all wetlands in Kruger, swimming, walking or clambering through aquatic vegetation in search of both plant and animal food.

The only potentially confusing species is the rare and erratic Lesser Moorhen (not illustrated), which is smaller and has a mostly yellow bill with red along the top.

☐ Black Crake L: 20 cm (8")

Crakes are waterside birds that creep in or beside dense vegetation or over small patches of mud. The Black Crake is small, rotund, almost tailless and entirely blackish except for its diagnostic bright pink-red legs, red-brown eye and yellowish bill. The immature is browner, with duller legs and bill. It is a common resident in almost all wet areas of Kruger where there is some cover into which it can retreat if disturbed, and the call is often heard – an odd wheezy bubbling and chattering *"cheeew-t-t-t-t treeew, t-t-t-t-t-treew"*. Prefers reedbeds and emergent vegetation on the edges of swamps and other waterbodies, where it forages, sometimes quite boldly. Like all crakes, its walks tentatively with its head lowered, picking and probing for invertebrates and plant matter. This crake is surprisingly aggressive and will kill other small birds it regards as competition. It will also scuttle over Hippopotamuses and Warthogs to remove parasites for food.

BLACK CRAKE IMMATURE

COMMON MOORHEN IMMATURE

RED-KNOBBED COOT IMMATURE

☐ Red-knobbed Coot L: 35–41 cm (14–16")

More duck-like than the Common Moorhen, this large, chicken-sized, black waterbird, is more often seen swimming than walking. It has a characteristic ivory-coloured bill and frontal shield, which is crested with two red-wine coloured knobs high on its head. These knobs expand in the breeding season. Common elsewhere in South Africa, it is a rare and erratic visitor to Kruger, where numbers may be greater in wetter years. It is very aggressive and will chase off much larger birds.

African Jacana L: 30 cm (12")

Somewhat resembling a long-legged moorhen (*page 38*), this is a chestnut, white and black waterbird, with a short, sky-blue bill and frontal shield, and very long legs. It trots on the surface of water lilies and other aquatic vegetation, with its ludicrously elongated toes preventing it from sinking. It flies weakly, low over the water, with legs and toes dangling behind awkwardly. The immature lacks the blue bill and shield of the adult, and is brown-headed. This is a common Kruger resident on dams, ponds and lakes where aquatic vegetation covers the water surface. It has a highly unusual mating system, with one dominant female maintaining a reverse harem of several males. After egg-laying the males each raise a brood alone. When there is danger, the chicks will run towards their father, who is able to tuck them under his wings and stand up and walk off with the whole brood protected.

VU ☐ African Finfoot   L: 66 cm (26")

An elongated, dark, duck-like aquatic bird with a bright orange bill and legs, the finfoot cannot easily be confused with anything else. Its back is spotted white, and the underparts are variably spotted and barred. The throat is grey on the male and white on the female. It swims slow and low in the water, with its tail held flat on the surface. The short, thick neck and bright bill differentiate it from the bulkier African Darter and cormorants (*pages 18–19*). African Finfoot is a rare resident in Kruger with a population of about 50–100 individuals. This highly secretive bird prefers rivers that flow year-round, such as the Levuvu, lower Olifants, Letaba, and Sabie Rivers. Pairs patrol quiet, clear backwaters, foraging under overhanging cover for invertebrates, frogs and fishes.

JUVENILE

MALE

FEMALE

41

☐ Water Thick-knee L: 40 cm (16")

Thick-knees are long-legged, plover-like birds, often resting inconspicuously by day. This species is similar to Spotted Thick-knee (*page 69*), but has greenish legs and a distinct black-edged grey panel across the wing – and, as its name suggests, favours more aquatic habitats. Up close it shows fine wavy streaks, rather than spots, on the back. The Water Thick-knee is common in Kruger, but never wanders far from permanent water, although it can occur in woodland adjacent to rivers, and even in camps. Although mostly nocturnal, it is also active at dawn and dusk, early evenings often being punctuated by its distinctive high-pitched, piping calls that speed up and then slow down again. It gives an open-winged threat display to startle predators, even sometimes successfully repelling monitor lizards. This thick-knee associates with Hippopotamuses and Nile Crocodiles, warning them of impending danger. In turn, the birds seem to benefit when crocodiles scare away monitors and other predators. Thick-knees are colloquially called 'dikkops', which in Afrikaans means 'thick-heads', a reference to their oversized domes.

NT ☐ **Greater Painted-Snipe** L: 25 cm (10")

A dumpy, colourful, snipe-like shorebird, with a slightly drooping bill, finely-barred brown back, white belly, and pale 'braces' extending over the shoulders. Unusually among birds, the female is more brightly coloured than the male, with a chestnut breast, nape and head, bolder head pattern, and pinkish bill. The male is more subdued, with olive-brown mottling, buffy-golden spectacles and eyestripe, horn-coloured bill and a sprinkling of golden spots over the wings. Painted-snipe are shy and inconspicuous birds that are scarce but regular along the muddy margins of wetlands and flooded grasslands throughout Kruger; numbers may increase in summer (December–March), and during wet years. The female's mournful "*wuuoo-uuuk*" call is sometime the first indication of their presence. Like the jacanas (*page 40*), each female will breed with several males.

MALE

FEMALE

Lapwings are tall, noisy, long-legged plovers that occur in both dry and wetland habitats.

☐ White-crowned Lapwing L: 32 cm (13")

This lapwing is identified by long yellow wattles, a white belly, and a grey head with a central white crown stripe. The back is brown, and the wings and tail are strikingly black-and-white, giving it a distinctive appearance, especially in flight. The superficially similar African Wattled Lapwing has a dark belly and red-based facial wattles. The White-crowned Lapwing gives a regularly repeated and characteristic high-pitched *"peek"* call. Although scarce in Kruger, numbering some 90 pairs, singles and pairs are conspicuous residents on large permanent rivers such as the Sabie, Levuvu and Limpopo. Birds forage for insects and small vertebrates almost exclusively along these riverbeds and the population in Kruger is being reduced by activities on river catchments outside the park.

WHITE-CROWNED LAPWING

BLACKSMITH LAPWING

AFRICAN WATTLED LAPWING

White-crowned Lapwing is slightly smaller than African Wattled Lapwing, has a white belly and lacks red at the base of the wattles.

☐ **Blacksmith Lapwing** L: 30 cm (12")

A striking grey, black and white lapwing, associated with water, this bird is boldly patterned, with a white crown and black face and breast, and dark legs. Immatures are browner than adults. A common breeding resident, it can be found at water bodies throughout Kruger and may also disperse into flooded grassland in the summer (December–March). It often draws attention with its namesake ringing *"tink"* calls uttered in series, like a blacksmith hammering on an anvil. A bold and brave parent, this bird has been known to charge African Elephants, or to harass raptors flying overhead, to protect its chicks.

☐ **African Wattled Lapwing** L: 34 cm (13")

A brown-bodied lapwing, with black-streaked throat and cheeks and white forehead, yellow facial wattles with distinctive fleshy red bases, and yellow legs. It has black-and-white wings and tail, but with brown on the inner wing extending to the bend. It is an uncommon resident in the southern half of Kruger, most frequently encountered in the Crocodile River valley; additional birds may visit from outside the park during the summer (December–March). Pairs or small groups can be found in marshes, wet grasslands or flooded edges of lakes, pans and seeps, attracting attention with loud *"peep-peep-peep"* calls.

Three-banded Plover is an abundant breeding resident that is present at almost every patch of water in Kruger.

☐ **Three-banded Plover** L: 18 cm (7")

A small, short-billed, brown-backed, white-bellied plover with two black breast-bands, grey cheeks, a white ring around the crown, and bright red skin around the eye and on the base of the bill. It is an abundant breeding resident that is present on almost every patch of water in Kruger. Calls *"weet-weet"* as it flies off when alarmed, showing prominent white sides to the long diamond-shaped tail, which it bobs upon landing. The call, tail-bobbing behaviour, and flight style are similar to those of Common Sandpiper.

☐ **Common Sandpiper** L: 19 cm (7·5")

This is a short-legged, slim-billed shorebird, with a hunched, horizontal carriage. It has a dark grey-brown back, greyish smudges on the breast, and an indistinct dark stripe through the eye and pale eyebrow. At close quarters you can see fine barring on the wings but more conspicuous is a white 'hook' beside the breast, curving up in front of the wing. It flies low over the water with bursts of rapid, shallow beats on stiffly bowed wings, showing a conspicuous white wingbar, a dark rump, and white along the edges of the tail, and often gives a ringing *"pee-weee"* call. Upon landing, and at other times, it characteristically bobs its hindquarters. A common spring and summer migrant (October–April) to many of Kruger's waterbodies, where it may even stand on the back of a semi-submerged Hippopotamus or Nile Crocodile when foraging.

☐ **Wood Sandpiper** L: 19 cm (7·5")

A medium-sized, elongated shorebird, with a strong white eyebrow extending behind the eye and a dark back spangled with buff-white spots. Its legs are long and yellow, and the straight bill is intermediate in length between Common Sandpiper and Common Greenshank (*page 48*). In flight it has uniform brown wings with no pale wingbar, and a square white rump. The underwings are pale, distinguishing it from the much rarer Green Sandpiper (not illustrated). Wood Sandpiper is perhaps the most common summer migrant (October–April) shorebird to freshwater habitats in Kruger, and is often detected by its distinctive high-pitched whistling *"chiff-iff-if"* calls in flight.

THREE-BANDED PLOVER

COMMION SANDPIPER

WOOD SANDPIPER

Common Greenshank L: 32 cm (13")

A rather large, greyish shorebird with long yellow-green legs, and a long, just perceptibly upturned two-tone bill that is greyish at the base and dark at the tip. In flight, a large white wedge extends from the rump to between the shoulders, and the wings are plain dark. The scarcer Marsh Sandpiper is similar, but smaller, more delicate, and has a needle-like bill. Common Greenshank is a common spring and summer visitor (October–April) to a variety of freshwater habitats, where it is usually the largest migrant shorebird present, walking deliberately on long legs and probing for food in the mud. It gives a distinctive loud, ringing *"teu-teu-teu"* call in flight.

Marsh Sandpiper L: 24 cm (9")

Marsh Sandpiper is rather like the Common Greenshank, but is smaller and more lightly built, with proportionately longer legs and an all-dark, needle-thin bill. In flight, it is also similar to Common Greenshank, with a large white wedge extending from the rump to between the shoulders, but the toes are more conspicuous, projecting farther beyond the end of the tail. Marsh Sandpiper is a scarce spring and summer migrant (October–April) in Kruger, where it prefers temporary wetlands and river edges, feeding on insects and other invertebrates. Its calls, *"tlit-tlit-tlit-tlit"*, are higher-pitched than those of Common Greenshank.

Black-winged Stilt L: 34 cm (13")

A distinctive black-backed, white bird, with red eyes, thin black needle-like bill and extremely long pink legs. Younger birds are browner on the back and have a white trailing edge to the wing. In flight, the adult shows a white wedge from the tail to the shoulders between black wings, and its long legs trail conspicuously, its feet often crossed. In the water it marches in goose-step fashion, lifting its legs high with long strides, while picking food from the surface. It is an uncommon resident in Kruger and can be found along any shallow still waters. Calls a high-pitched *"kik-kik-kik"*.

IMMATURE

ADULT

49

LITTLE STINT

CURLEW SANDPIPER

RUFF

◻ **Little Stint** L: 14 cm (5·5")

A tiny, short-legged, straight-billed, grey-brown shorebird. Small size, black legs and bill, and variable dusky streaking on the breast sides distinguish it from Kruger's other regular shorebirds. It is significantly smaller than Curlew Sandpiper and has a short, straight (not drooping) bill, and tends to keep to shallower water or wet mud. It is fast and active, with constantly moving feet. Although it is an uncommon spring and summer visitor (October–April) to Kruger, all other very small shorebirds are vagrants, so the Little Stint is far the most likely to be encountered. It gives a simple *"tit-it"* call.

◻ **Ruff** L: 22–32 cm (9–13")

This medium-sized, pot-bellied, pale brownish shorebird has a small head, longish neck and relatively short bill, giving it a 'gravy-boat' appearance. Males are much larger than females. Orange legs and bill base are characteristic on adults (the legs may be redder on males), although immature birds have more greenish-ochre legs. In flight it has an indistinct wingbar, and a white diagonal stripe on each side of the tail. The wingbeats are deep and slow, giving it a languid flight action. An uncommon and erratic spring and summer visitor (October–April) to freshwater habitats within Kruger, normally feeding on mudflats, but sometimes swimming in a spinning motion. Its scientific name Philomachus pugnax means 'the combative battle-lover', and refers to the intense fights between males on the lekking and breeding grounds in northern Eurasia. At that season, males have colourful ruffs that give the bird its common name, but this plumage is not seen in Kruger.

◻ **Curlew Sandpiper** L: 20 cm (8")

A small, plain, greyish-backed, waterside sandpiper, with a distinctive long, drooping bill. The prominent white eyebrow fades behind the eye, and in flight the bird has a characteristic white rump patch and thin white wingbars. Wood Sandpiper (*page 46*) is taller, with a straight bill and spangled back, and plain wings above a broader white rump; Common Sandpiper (*page 46*) bobs and has a darker back, and shows white wing stripes in flight. An uncommon spring and summer visitor (October–April) to Kruger, using a variety of wetland habitats, often wading up to its belly and probing downwards as it feeds. It gives a slightly rippling *"chirrup"* call.

LITTLE STINT

RUFF

CURLEW SANDPIPER

Kingfishers are large-headed, long-billed, short-tailed and short-legged birds that perch upright; some, but not all, are associated with water (see *pages 94–95* for the non-aquatic kingfishers).

☐ Pied Kingfisher L: 25 cm (10")

This is a large, crested, black-and-white, water-loving kingfisher. The male has two complete black bands across the upper chest; the female has a single broken band. An explosive metallic chattering draws attention to pairs and small groups, which are commonly encountered on Kruger's waterbodies.

Pied Kingfishers are excellent fish hunters, seeking prey from perches or by hovering over the water, but they will also eat invertebrates. They dig nests in riverbanks, either solitarily or in loose colonies, and can breed co-operatively. Helpers from the previous year's breeding attempt assist the adults with feeding and territory defence, which significantly improves the chicks' chances of survival. Nests are sometimes raided by snakes, monitors and Water Mongoose.

MALE

FEMALE

☐ Malachite Kingfisher L: 14 cm (5·5")

This is a tiny, dazzling kingfisher – an ultramarine and orange jewel with a red bill. It is always found close to water, unlike the similar African Pygmy-Kingfisher (not illustrated), which favours woodland and differs in its head coloration: lilac ear patch and an orange eyebrow. It is a common resident, usually seen perched on a rush or reed along the edge of a waterbody, normally less than a metre above the water's surface. Hunts from a perch and can only penetrate the upper few centimetres of the water, where it takes fishes, tadpoles and invertebtates.

PIED KINGFISHER

GIANT KINGFISHER

FEMALE

■ Giant Kingfisher L: 44 cm (17")

A very large, chunky, black, white and chestnut kingfisher, with a huge, dagger-like black bill and small crest. Sexes differ in the positioning of the chestnut: on the male it is on the upper breast; on the female the chestnut is on the belly, vent and underwing coverts. This kingfisher is a conspicuous resident on large rivers and wetlands throughout Kruger, often drawing attention with raucous and rapidly repeated "*kek*" and "*kakh*" calls. It often hunts crabs, dismembering them with its large bill, but will also take fishes, frogs and invertebrates.

MALE

Yellow-throated Longclaw L: 21 cm (8")

This bulky, pipit-like ground bird has golden-yellow underparts and eyebrows, with a circular, broad black necklace emphasising its bright yellow throat. The upperparts are a subdued streaky pale brown but the outermost corners of the tail are white, a key feature in flight. It is a fairly common resident throughout Kruger, preferring wet grasslands, where it often perches in the open, singing a strongly whistled *"chuuu-ew"* and variations. Longclaws feed mainly on invertebrates on the ground. When alarmed, they will turn their back to the threat, becoming remarkably well camouflaged, despite the vivid coloration of the underparts.

Longclaws are colourful relatives of the sombre pipits. While pipits prefer open habitats, the longclaws frequent thicker, wet grassland, where they construct their grass nests on the ground.

☐ **African Pied Wagtail** L: 20 cm (8")

Africa's only all black-and-white wagtail,
showing a bold white eyebrow and wing
panels, and a broad black throat patch.
The brown juvenile may resemble the
locally rare Cape Wagtail (not illustrated),
but unlike that species has extensive white
panels in the wings. Although streams,
dams and riverine fringes are the preferred
habitat, it wanders far from water and is
a common resident throughout Kruger.
African Pied Wagtails strut along the
margins of wetlands or over rest camp
lawns, searching for invertebrates; they
can change direction suddenly, using their
long 'wagging' tails for balance and poise.

In Zambia the African Pied Wagtail is
protected from persecution, as traditional
beliefs suggest that it is the reincarnation
of a small child that has died.

JUVENILE

ADULT

☐ Tawny-flanked Prinia L: 13 cm (5")

An active little warbler-like bird with mouse-brown upperparts and pale underparts, and a long, graduated tail that is frequently cocked, waved and flicked. Close views will reveal an indistinct pale eyebrow, dark line through the eye, rufous-brown flight feathers and rump, black bill and brownish eye. This is a common breeding resident throughout Kruger, preferring grassy thickets and riverine scrub and frequently joins large mixed flocks. Calls a loud, repeated *"chweet-chweet-chweeet"* and also gives tinny *"stip-stip-stip"* calls.

☐ Red-faced Cisticola L: 14 cm (5·5")

Cisticolas are all very small warbler-like birds (see *page 129* for other, more terrestrial, cisticolas). The Red-faced Cisticola is a relatively large species, appearing plain grey-buff, lacking the streaking shown by most other cisticolas, and has warm rufous cheeks, especially in spring and summer (October–March). It is most often detected and easily identified by its loud ringing whistle, *"whe-whe-chee-chee-chee-cheer-cheer-cheer-cheer"*. In Kruger this species is widespread and fairly common in its favoured habitat of tall, thick grass alongside rivers and wetlands, such as at Letaba camp.

☐ **Burchell's Coucal** L: 41 cm (16")

Coucals are large, robust, cuckoos with stout, arched bills. This species has creamy-white underparts, chestnut wings and back, and is glossy-black on the head and tail. Often perches up on reeds or bushes, clambers heavily through vegetation, or walks on the ground in a rather ungainly fashion on short legs. It is a common resident throughout Kruger, except in the far north, such as along the Limpopo and Levuvu rivers, where it is mostly replaced by the White-browed Coucal (not illustrated but told by its prominent white eyebrow). The female displays and makes a deep descending series of "*bu-bu-bu bu bu bu bu*" calls that fall and then rise, sometimes answered by the male. The male builds the nest, incubates the eggs and plays the major role in rearing the young. Burchell's Coucal is a rapacious predator of insects, small mammals and reptiles, and will raid other birds' nests.

☐ Common Ostrich L: 1·9 m (6 ft)

This enormous, long-legged and long-necked flightless bird – the world's largest – is easily identified by size alone. Males have black and white feathers, and pink-flushed skin when breeding; females have grey-brown plumage. The Common Ostrich is uncommon and widespread in open grasslands and sparse woodlands, but commonest in Kruger's eastern plains, especially north of Letaba. Gives a deep booming call like a distant Lion's roar, *"hooo booo hoooomph hooo"*, that can be heard kilometres away. Ostriches have a complex breeding system with one 'alpha' female and several subordinates laying 15–30 eggs in the same nest, the chicks subsequently forming large crèches.

Zulus call the Ostrich the 'renewer' because the fat, boiled and mixed with ochre, was used to protect skin, bring dreams and visions of the future, and to act as a burial agent to help transport people to the spiritual world. Ostrich eggs were also thought to be an aphrodisiac amongst Khoi-khoi men.

FEMALE

MALE

CHICKS

☐ Cattle Egret

L: 56 cm (22") | WS: 88–96 cm (35–38")

The smallest and dumpiest white egret, with a
short, compressed neck and rather short legs.
Breeding adults have a yellow bill and legs,
and a diagnostic honey-coloured hue to their
head and breast. Non-breeding and immature
birds have darker legs, but the bill remains
yellow, unlike that of the Little Egret (*page 23*).
Generally an uncommon resident and nomad
(although numbers are increasing in southern
Kruger) occurring singly or in small groups in
grassland, bush or wetland. Flocks often associate
with large mammals such as buffalos, wildebeests
and elephants, feeding on insects flushed by the
animals as they move. Occasionally seen riding
on the back of mammals, especially where the
vegetation is dense.

BREEDING

☐ Hadeda Ibis L: 76 cm (30")

A medium-sized brown bird with an iridescent
green-purple gloss on the wings, the Hadeda
Ibis has a distinctive downcurved bill – black
underneath with red at the base of the upper
mandible – and a characteristic white streak
across the cheeks under the eye. It is common
and widespread in open habitats in Kruger.
The frequently heard call is one of the most
evocative sounds of Africa – a loud, raucous,
trumpeting *"ha-da-da"*, which gives the bird its
name. Arrival and departure from tree roosts are
normally accompanied by much raucous calling,
often to the irritation of local people who have
little option but to put up with the cacophony.
Birds forage on the ground, digging and picking
up invertebrates with their long bill.

CATTLE EGRET

NON-BREEDING

HADEDA IBIS

☐ Black-headed Heron L: 92 cm (36") | WS: 150 cm (59")

A typical heron in shape, this mostly grey bird with a distinct black cap and white throat (although juveniles are duskier) is a dry-land species. It resembles a juvenile Grey Heron (*page 21*), but has slate-grey rather than yellowish legs and a darker bill. At all ages the underwing pattern is much more strongly two-toned than on Grey Heron, with pale forewings contrasting with black flight feathers. An uncommon but widespread resident in Kruger, this heron is usually found away from water, happily foraging in burnt grassland or open savannah, although it may also occasionally haunt a pond or quiet river bend.

ADULT

ADULT

IMMATURE

NT ☐ **Abdim's Stork**   L: 73 cm (29") | WS: 140 cm (55")

A relatively small, dark stork, with blackish wings, back and neck, and a white belly. The legs are greyish, with distinctive pink-red feet and knees, the bill is greyish, and the facial skin bluish and red. Abdim's Stork could be confused with the rarer and more solitary Black Stork (not illustrated), but is smaller, has a white rump, and dull rather than bright red legs and bill. It is a non-breeding intra-African migrant and is rare in some years but abundant in others, present during spring and summer (October–April), when huge flocks can be found around insect irruptions as the summer rains intensify.

Wetland storks are covered on *pages 26–28*

NT ☐ **Marabou Stork** L: 152 cm (60") | WS: 300–370 cm (118–146")

This huge, slaty-backed, white-bellied stork has a massive
dagger-like bill and a naked pink head and neck that appears
severely sunburned. A white ruff and loose inflatable skin on
the neck add to its odd appearance and separate it from other
storks. Most of the South African population, some 400 birds,
occurs scattered across Kruger, mainly as non-breeding visitors.
This stork is an excellent flier and is able to soar effortlessly at
great heights searching for food; its wingspan exceeds that
of most vultures. It has a highly varied diet and will eat
almost anything: birds have even been recorded eating
shoes and metal at garbage dumps! Marabous are
equally content in wetlands and in dry bush, but
are most frequently encountered lurking
on the margins of kills, where they
opportunistically snatch carrion.
On hot days they defecate onto
their legs for evaporative
cooling (a habit known
as urohidrosis), staining
them whitish.

☐ White Stork L: 115 cm (45") | WS: 155–215 cm (61–85")

A large, white-and-black bird with long red legs, a long neck, and a straight, dagger-like red bill. In flight it is mostly white with a broad black trailing edge to the wings above and below. Juvenile birds are dingier. This is a spring and summer migrant (October–April) to Kruger, where it often occurs in open grasslands in small- to medium-sized flocks. It soars expertly, using thermals to gain height, often in wheeling flocks. White Storks eat mostly insects, but will also take reptiles, birds and small mammals. They regularly forage in association with ungulates, which flush prey, and occur with other birds, including Abdim's Storks (*page 61*), at insect emergences.

The White Stork is revered across its Eurasian breeding range as the 'bringer of babies', and by Muslims for this migrant's tendency to make an annual pilgrimage to Mecca!

☐ Swainson's Spurfowl

L: 33–38 cm (13–15")

Spurfowl are rounded, chicken-like ground birds in the francolin group. This is a large, brown species, with some darker streaks, black legs, and distinctive bare red facial skin and throat patch. It is common in Kruger, and bold and conspicuous, standing on open branches and termite mounds to give its loud *"kreeeeet-kreeeeet-kreeeet"* call in the early morning and at dusk.

The Swainson's Spurfowl is highly dependent upon water, so if you are looking for one check the dams or rivers in the early morning or late evening.

☐ Helmeted Guineafowl

L: 53–60 cm (21–24")

Guineafowl are large-bodied, small-headed, slaty-grey ground birds, adorned with perfect rows of hundreds of white spots. The Helmeted Guineafowl has a distinctive head, with naked warty blue-and-red facial skin and a strange, upstanding, bone-like casque. Young birds are all-brown, and almost always in the company of adults. The darker Crested Guineafowl (*page 164*) lacks a casque and is mostly found in the far north of the park. Helmeted Guineafowl is a common to abundant resident, with large flocks roaming the bush, digging and scratching for invertebrates and tubers to eat. Birds often behave erratically, charging around making loud, harsh *"kek-kek-kek-kraaaaaaah"* alarm calls. Males frequently fight, charging at each other with their head lowered and wings raised.

One of the BIG 6

NT ☐ **Kori Bustard** L: 120–150 cm (47–59") | WS: 230–275 cm (91–108")

Bustards are stout-billed ground birds with long, thick legs. In flight, they reveal long, fingered wings and fly with their necks outstretched. The Kori Bustard is the largest bustard and has a black crest, a long greyish neck, brown back and black-and-white dappling on the bend of the wing. Among Kruger's birds, it is second only to the Common Ostrich (*page 58*) in size, weighing 7–18 kg. Although it is uncommon, with a population of 100–250 individuals, due to its massive size and preference for open areas, it is a conspicuous species that is encountered regularly in the grassier open woodlands of Kruger. Although Kori Bustards rarely fly, when they do so, they remain low, flapping with slow and shallow wing beats; large males are among the heaviest flying birds in the world. Singles and pairs march slowly and purposefully across the savannah, picking large insects, small vertebrates and plant material off the ground and low bushes. Males make an almost inaudible low-frequency *"doop"* sound – like a base drum – that travels a great distance. They display in loose groups at leks, puffing out their throat plumes and cocking their tails like turkeys, making their necks look like giant white feather-dusters that can be visible at great distances. They also fight, pushing each other, charging and stabbing with their bills, to establish dominance. Several females mate with the most impressive male, thereafter departing to nest and raising their young alone.

Kori Bustards are known to follow antelope, preying on animals they disturb – and, in turn, are used as perches by bee-eaters and drongos, which feed on what the bustard itself flushes. Many predators hunt Kori Bustards, the most frequent being the huge Martial Eagle (*page 188*). Kori Bustards have the unusual ability to suck up, rather than scoop, water to drink.

☐ Crowned Lapwing
L: 30 cm (12")

Lapwings are medium-sized ground birds with long legs, short bills and broad, rounded wings. The Crowned Lapwing is tall and brown with a white belly, and has a distinct white 'halo' ring around a dark crown. The immature is duller, but still retains the crown pattern. This species is common in Kruger, including some of the camps, with numbers increasing in the winter (June–August) when grasslands are more open. Small groups feed in cropped and recently burnt grassland, where they search for their favoured prey, termites and ants. Noisy, scratchy "*kirre*" calls give it the Afrikaans name of Kiwiet.

☐ Senegal Lapwing L: 26 cm (10")

An upright, white-bellied, dark lapwing with a grey breast and face, white chin and forehead, and black legs. It differs from the superficially similar Black-winged Lapwing (not illustrated) by its smaller size, dark legs, a distinct small white forehead patch, and, in flight, by an all-white trailing edge to the wing. Senegal Lapwing is somewhat nomadic, although its movements are poorly understood, and is uncommon in Kruger, while Black-winged Lapwing has not been confirmed to occur in the park. Small groups scurry on open, gravelly and short-grass plains looking for insects, and it is frequently found in recently burnt grasslands. Its presence can be detected by loud "*chi-whoo*" calls.

☐ Spotted Thick-knee L: 43 cm (17")

A tall, tawny-brown, yellow-legged terrestrial bird, a little like a large plover and resembling the Water Thick-knee (*page 42*), but with distinct dark spots. Its huge yellow eyes hint at its mainly nocturnal habits: by day this strange-looking bird crouches down under bushes or other cover and uses its cryptic plumage to conceal itself; after dark it becomes active and runs around feeding on insects. Spotted Thick-knee is an uncommon resident in Kruger, and is often seen on night drives; groups may reveal their presence with loud *"ti-ti-ti teeeteeeteeee-ti ti ti"* calls. If an intruder approaches a nest the adult bird engages in an elaborate threat display, drooping its wings, extending its neck, and charging forward, hissing loudly. The Afrikaans name for thick-knees is 'dikkop', which means 'thick-head' – a reference to the bulbous head.

When sleeping during the day, the Spotted Thick-knee is cryptic and can be difficult to find. It crouches down, often appearing horizontal, with its breast, neck and head flush to the ground and its legs covered. Look under bushes and in shaded areas if you are trying to find one.

Hoopoes are so distinctive that they are placed in their own family, but are fairly closely related to woodhoopoes (*page 102*).

☐ African Hoopoe L: 28 cm (11")

A ground-hugging, buffy-orange, black and white bird, with a thin, downcurved bill. It has a broad, fan-like crest which is occasionally raised, but often laid flat. The flight action is slow and undulating, low to the ground with jerky beats of rounded black-and-white striped wings. The African Hoopoe is a common resident in Kruger and often frequents camp lawns. It shuffles on short legs using its bill to probe soft soil, dry leaves or animal dung in search of invertebrate food. Its famous trick is to mimic an ant, using its fine bill to trickle grains of sand into an antlion burrow. When the antlion comes to the surface the hunter becomes the hunted, and a handy hoopoe snack. The name hoopoe is derived from the bird's distinctive *"hoop-poop-poop"* call, often given from a perch in a tree.

In South African folklore, the presence of a hoopoe is a welcome sign, suggesting you will soon have a visit from a loyal friend.

☐ Double-banded Sandgrouse L: 25 cm (10")

Sandgrouse are plump, small-headed, short-billed, dove-like, terrestrial birds. This species looks brown at a distance, but a close view reveals subtly beautiful patterning and a yellow eye-ring. The male is distinguished from the female by its bright orange bill, above which there are bold black and white bars. A fairly common resident, it prefers patches of short tussocky and recently burnt grassland near rocky areas in woodland, particularly Mopane thicket. It is often found alongside roads, and when not moving its cryptic plumage makes it an easy bird to overlook. Double-banded Sandgrouse is largely inactive by day, preferring to forage at night, and just before and after twilight. Birds call a bubbling *"oh NO, he's gone and done it AGAIN"*, particularly when arriving at a waterhole to drink. Sandgrouse have the remarkable habit of synchronously coming to water in large numbers at dusk, gathering at a sort of 'secret ceremony', where they drink, call and socialise briefly before dispersing.

☐ Zitting Cisticola L: 11 cm (4·5")

One of the small, streaky, brown cisticolas, this is a tiny, short-tailed, warbler-like bird with pale spots on the tip of the tail. It is a fairly common and widespread resident of Kruger's grasslands, where it forages low down for small invertebrates. This aptly named cisticola is most often detected and identified by its incessant, metallic *"zit. . . zit. . . zit"* call, which is often given in a display flight, synchronised with deep undulations, especially in spring and summer (October–March). The similar Desert Cisticola (not illustrated) is less common, prefers drier areas, and has a more complicated, less monotonous song.

FEMALE

☐ Chestnut-backed Sparrowlark
L: 13 cm (5")

This small bird is aptly named, being a ground-loving lark in behaviour but shaped more like a small sparrow. The male is a striking white-eared, chestnut-backed, black-bellied bird; the female is more subdued but still shows a characteristic black belly, pale nape patch and chestnut back. It is a common resident, mainly in the eastern half of Kruger, but it is locally nomadic with numbers increasing when favoured grasses produce abundant seed.

MALE

ZITTING CISTICOLA

☐ Rufous-naped Lark
L: 15–18 cm (6–7")

Larks are small- to medium-sized ground birds that walk and run, rather than hop (as do finches) or cling to upright stems (like bishops and whydahs). This is a large, robust, rust-coloured lark, with a short crest and a hefty bill. Rufous-naped Lark is a common resident of the grassy savannahs and woodlands, particularly in eastern Kruger, where it forages on the ground for small insects and seeds. It is most conspicuous in the spring and summer (October–March) when it perches up, singing a sweet *"treee-leee-treeloo"*, occasionally drooping its wings and jumping with a small flutter. It may also fly up, exposing the broad rufous wings that it shares with the much smaller and scarcer Flappet Lark (not illustrated).

☐ African Pipit L: 17 cm (6·5")

A medium-sized, slender pipit with long legs, told from larks by its longer tail and slimmer bill, and from other similar species by its habit of walking rather than hopping on the ground. Although it appears very plain from a distance, a close view reveals a bold pale eyebrow and moustache, a streaky back and a band of streaking across the chest, but otherwise pale unmarked underparts. The long, slender bill is dark with a yellowish base. The much smaller and scarcer Bushveld Pipit (*page 122*) has a short tail and plainer face. Plain-backed and Buffy Pipits (neither illustrated) also occur in Kruger but are much rarer: both are unstreaked on the back and have buff rather than white outer tail feathers. The African Pipit is an abundant resident throughout Kruger, where it favours short grass plains and stubble.

☐ Wattled Starling L: 21 cm (8")

Starlings are stout, sharp-billed, strong-legged birds that often walk and run along the ground. Wattled Starling is grey-brown with dark wings and tail, and a whitish rump. The pale bill and lemon-yellow facial skin in females and non-breeding males is subdued, but breeding males acquire long, fleshy, dangling wattles with naked, canary-yellow skin on the face, making them unmistakable. This gregarious nomad is almost always found in groups, and breeds colonially, sometimes sharing nests with weavers. It is irregular and irruptive in Kruger's grasslands and open savannahs – in some years numbering in the thousands, yet in others being almost absent. Sometimes associates with large mammals, feeding on insects that are flushed. Both sexes give a variety of squeaks and hissing notes.

WATTLED STARLING
NON–BREEDING

☐ Familiar Chat L: 15 cm (6")

This dumpy, plain-brown bird has rusty ear patches and rufous on the rump and outer tail feathers. The juvenile is spotted and scaled buff. Birds frequently flick their wings and lift their tail – behaviours that are usually sufficient to confirm identification. This species is uncommon but widespread in Kruger, favouring rocky areas and buildings, where it often perches conspicuously. Its main food is invertebrates, and birds have been recorded associating with Klipspringers, catching insects that they flush.

BREEDING

◻ **African Stonechat** L: 14 cm (5·5")

This chat is a small, dumpy, upright and short-tailed bird that sits prominently on grasses, bushes or twigs. The male has a chestnut breast, black head, back and tail, and a white rump, and a diagnostic large white patch on the side of the neck and a shoulder stripe. The female is orange-buff underneath, mottled grey-brown above and has a dull buff eyebrow. This bird is a fairly common, but conspicuous, winter visitor to Kruger (May–August), when it inhabits open grasslands with scattered shrubs. It has a habit of swooping down to catch an insect before returning to a favourite perch.

The scientific name of this bird, *Saxicola torquatus*, refers to its appearance and habitat preference. The name is is derived from Latin words and has the meaning 'collared rock-dweller' – *Saxicola* from *saxum* ('rock') + *incola* ('one who dwells in a place') and *torquatus* ('collared').

FEMALE

MALE

This was the Zulu King Shaka's favourite bird, which he called 'the scatterer of enemies'. The feathers were worn into battle only by the fiercest warriors, who would rather die than return home defeated.

☐ Magpie Shrike L: 45 cm (18")

This long-tailed, bulky, shrike is mostly black but has prominent white patches. Small groups of 3–10 sit upright on perches in open areas where they pounce on, hawk and glean a wide range of invertebrate prey. It is common and widespread throughout Kruger, with a population estimated at 16,000 birds, but particularly numerous in the eastern grasslands. They may move locally in response to fire and drought. Calls a shrill starling- or parrot-like "*pleeee-eouuu*" given by more than one bird, and also gives harsh grating cries.

Shrikes are large-headed, long-tailed birds with stout, slightly hooked bills. They hunt from perches, watching vigilantly for insects and other invertebrates, before pouncing on them and returning to a perch. Prey is occasionally cached by being impaled on thorns for later consumption.

☐ Red-backed Shrike L: 17 cm (6·5")

This small shrike has very different male and female plumages: males have a small, black 'bandit's' face-mask, a grey head and rump, reddish-brown back and wings, pink underside and a black-and-white tail; females are plainer with a dark brown back, wings and tail, an ashy-brown crown and a much weaker mask. Although it breeds across Eurasia, most of the world population migrates to southern Africa and it is a common summer visitor (November–April) to Kruger. Here it favours open thornveld, with males seeming to prefer foraging in more open areas, while females concentrate in thicker groves. When agitated birds jerk their tail from side to side.

FEMALE

MALE

☐ Lesser Grey Shrike L: 21 cm (8")

A large-headed, upright shrike: adults are strikingly patterned grey, black and white and have a broad black mask continuing up over the forehead; juveniles are scaly and lack the black forehead. This is a fairly common summer visitor (November–April) to Kruger, favouring the eastern grasslands and arid woodlands. During the northern hemisphere winter, virtually the entire world population migrates from Eurasia to southern Africa. Departure for the breeding grounds is remarkably synchronous, as millions of birds vacate southern Africa in just a few nights in early April.

Crested Francolin
L: 30–35 cm (12–14")

A medium-sized, buff-brown francolin with a bushy crest that is sometimes raised, and a broad, 'string-of-pearls' collar around the white throat. It is a common and widespread resident, often found at picnic areas and in riverine woodland, walking confidently with a cocked tail – giving it a chicken-like gait. Birds herald dawn and dusk with a repeated series of rapid, cheery *"cheer kirk-kik"* calls, usually given as a synchronised duet between a pair – one of Kruger's most distinctive and characteristic wild sounds.

Around their dens, African Wild Dogs have developed a surprising tolerance of Crested Francolins – perhaps because the birds' alarm calls provide the dogs with early warning of dangerous predators such as Spotted Hyenas and Lions.

Coqui Francolin
L: 20–28 cm (8–11")

The Coqui Francolin is small, males having a distinctive rusty head and black and white bars on the breast and belly; females are duller, with a small black crescent extending from the eyebrow to the upper neck, and a black-bordered white throat. The rare Shelley's Francolin (not illustrated) looks similar to the female Coqui Francolin but has strong rufous streaking on the underparts. An uncommon and secretive resident, the Coqui Francolin prefers to remain hidden in tall grass, where it is most often detected by its characteristic calls: a di-syllabic, repetitive *"ko-kwi, ko-kwi"* and an accelerating *"ter-ink, tara-tara-tara"*.

FEMALE

MALE

Natal Spurfowl   L: 30–38 cm (12–15")

A medium-sized, brownish francolin with distinctive yellow nostrils and bright orange-red bill and legs. The back is mottled brown, and the underparts are finely barred brown and white, giving a marbled appearance. Juveniles have a similar plumage to adults, but the legs and bill are duller. This is a common resident in Kruger, and although it prefers thick undergrowth some birds have become bold scroungers at various camps and picnic areas. The call is a loud, raucous *"kak-kreek"* that variably accelerates and decelerates.

Natal Spurfowl feed mainly on plants during the winter (June–August), but at other times of the year their diet is supplemented with invertebrates.

Natal Spurfowl tend to be most active at dawn and dusk, usually retiring to dense cover during the heat of the day. They are sometimes seen dust bathing in open areas close to thickets.

☐ Red-crested Korhaan L: 50 cm (20")

MALE IN DISPLAY

Korhaans are small bustards that walk stealthily on the ground;
the Red-crested Korhaan has a black belly and diagnostic white
chevrons on a brown-and-black-mottled back. The male has
a brown-grey neck and slaty cap, while the female is plainer.
Only males have the red crest and this is almost always hidden.
In flight it has an all-black underwing – Black-bellied Bustard
has white panels in the underwing. It is a common resident in Kruger's drier woodlands.
Males have a distinctive song: a sequence of clicking *"tic-tic"* notes followed by a
mournful piping series, *"sweee-swee-sweee sweet"* that accelerates to a crescendo. They
will mate with several females and are not involved in nest care or parenting. They also
indulge in an absurd display, flying almost vertically into the sky, then folding their wings
and tumbling down as if shot, before surprisingly landing on their feet. Korhaans are
preyed upon by several large eagles, and are sometimes taken by mammalian predators
such as Leopards.

FEMALE

MALE

☐ Black-bellied Bustard L: 58–65 cm (23–26")

A large, lithe, bustard with black daubs on a mostly tan-coloured back. The male has a black belly, neck stripe, throat and face patch, but the female is uniform buff-brown from belly to head. In flight, males have a large white panel near the wingtip, whereas females have a series of white spots – the presence of white separating this species from the Red-crested Korhaan. It is an uncommon resident in tall grassland and grassy savannah, although seems to vacate the northern part of Kruger in summer (December–March). The male's strange display involves stretching his neck upwards and making a frog-like "*kwoork*" croak as he retracts his head into the shoulders, like a guilty child, followed by a "*grrrr*" growl and champagne-cork "*pop*" as it lifts it again. This looks as ridiculous as it sounds! Males also perform an aerial display with the wings held back rigidly, and with its throat puffed out. This bustard occasionally falls prey to Martial Eagles (*page 188*) and Leopards.

FEMALE

MALE

81

Although the dove is a symbol of peace in many countries, in some African traditional cultures doves are thought to be quite villainous, as males are willing to kill each other for the attentions of a female. There are several similar-looking doves in Kruger that are worth getting to know.

MALE

FEMALE

NAMAQUA DOVE

LAUGHING DOVE

EMERALD-SPOTTED WOOD-DOVE

☐ Namaqua Dove L: 26 cm (10")

This small-bodied, greyish dove has a distinctively long, slender, pointed tail. The male has a black throat and red-and-yellow bill, although these are lacking in the female. In its dashing flight, the combination of reddish wings and long 'pin-tail' are diagnostic. The Namaqua Dove is nomadic, being common to abundant in dry years and rare in wet years. It prefers the drier western portions of Kruger, particularly thornveld. The call is a mournful, strained *"whooooo"* given up to 20 times in succession.

☐ Laughing Dove L: 25 cm (10")

An elegant, long-tailed, slender, dark pink dove with a coppery mantle and slate blue-grey outer wings, rump and central tail feathers. It lacks the 'collar' which is a feature of some other doves (see *pages 84–85*), but has a stippled black necklace and white-and-black outer tail feathers that are distinctive in flight. This is an abundant resident in Kruger, with pairs and small groups found in all habitats. A low, chuckling *"croo-doo-doo-doo-doo"* song gives the bird its name. Males launch into the air with loud wing-clapping, and then glide down in a gentle arc – one of the characteristic signs of spring.

☐ Emerald-spotted Wood-Dove L: 20 cm (8")

A small, dainty, pinkish-grey, ground-dwelling dove, with a pale crown and two rows of iridescent green spots on the wing. The all-dark bill (not yellow and red) and colour of the wing spots (green rather than blue) differentiate it from the much rarer Blue-spotted Wood-Dove (not illustrated). In flight it reveals bright rufous wings and two grey bands across the back and one across the tail. This is a common if somewhat inconspicuous resident throughout Kruger, preferring drier woodlands, and the characteristic call is a familiar Kruger sound: it starts tentatively and mournfully drops in pitch before gently fading away: *"duuuuh-duuuueh, duueh-dduuue-due-due-due-due-dueh, do-do-do-do-do-do-do-do"*. This call is interpreted by Shangaan people as *"My mother is dead, my father is dead, and now my heart just goes du-du-du-du-du-du-du"*.

MALE

NAMAQUA DOVE

FEMALE

LAUGHING DOVE

EMERALD-SPOTTED WOOD-DOVE

Kruger has three common, plain-looking doves with broad black collars around their necks. They differ subtly, and are worth learning early in a visit.

RED-EYED DOVE   CAPE TURTLE DOVE

☐ Red-eyed Dove L: 35 cm (14")

The largest and stockiest 'collared' dove, with a pale-fronted, pinkish head and dark red eye. In flight, the dirty-brown tail tips distinguish it from other 'collared' doves. It is an abundant resident, especially in camps and picnic sites, and has an insistent and characteristic song *"I AM a red-eyed dove"*. It feeds on seeds and other plant matter on the ground.

☐ African Mourning Dove L: 30 cm (12")

Similar to Red-eyed Dove, but smaller, with a dusky grey head, and a diagnostic yellow eye surrounded by bare red skin. In flight it shows white in the outer tail. Although common, it is the least abundant of Kruger's collared doves, preferring wet, wooded areas. This dove is particularly common alongside human habitations in well-treed areas such as Shingwedzi, Letaba, Satara and other camps. It gives a distinctive *"Look AT me"* song, and a variety of crooning, throaty *"craaaooow"* sounds, particularly at the climax of an aerial display flight with wings and tail spread in a slow, parachuting descent.

☐ Cape Turtle Dove L: 28 cm (11")

This is the smallest and greyest collared dove, which has a small, gentle-looking black eye that is not surrounded by any bare red skin. It has a pale belly and shows broad white tips and sides to the tail in flight. The Cape Turtle Dove is an abundant resident throughout Kruger, its incessant *"work HAR-der, work HAR-der"* song, repeated every few seconds, being a common and characteristic sound of the African bush.

RED-EYED DOVE

AFRICAN MOURNING DOVE

CAPE TURTLE DOVE

Go-away-birds can often be seen perched on top of bushes, while cuckoos, with their short, slightly curved bills, rather long wings and long tails, may be inconspicuous deep inside tree canopies. The calls are an excellent clue to their presence.

☐ Grey Go-away-bird L: 50 cm (20")

A slender, long-tailed and long-necked ash-grey bird, with a crest that can be raised or laid flat, a chunky black bill and a beady dark eye. It forms small groups and is abundant in drier woodlands throughout Kruger, where it is estimated to number more than 65,000 individuals. The well-known nasal *"guuu-waaaay"* or *"kwee"* calls are often answered by others nearby. Birds clamber with considerable agility through vegetation, foraging on fruit, flowers, buds and insects, but fly with floppy wing beats. They will mob owls, goshawks, eagles and even mammalian predators, raising their crest, calling agitatedly and bouncing around.

Much revered by some traditional cultures, the go-away-bird is believed to be able to see evil spirits called 'tokoloshes' and chastise them until they depart.

Red-chested Cuckoo L: 30 cm (12″)

This is a slaty-backed and grey-headed cuckoo with dark bars on the underparts, and a broad, rusty band across the upper breast (palest in females); immatures have a charcoal-grey back, throat and breast, with barred underparts. It is a common spring and summer visitor (September–April) to Kruger, its presence revealed by an incessant, loud, three-note song *"Piet-my-wife"* or *"it will rain"*, although it can be frustratingly difficult to see. The Red-chested Cuckoo flies fast on pointed wings, strongly resembling a small goshawk (*pages 196–198*). This clever piece of trickery may cause birds to flee their nests in fear, providing the cuckoo with an opportunity to locate the nest, lay an egg, and remove one of the host's eggs without being detected. The parasitized bird then rears the young cuckoo. Hosts include wagtails, robin-chats and thrushes.

The Famous French naturalist Francois Levaillant worked with a collecting assistant named Piet. The story goes that upon collecting a female Red-chested Cuckoo, Piet was haunted by a male bird that followed and scolded him for his dastardly act, constantly singing "Piet-my-wife".

☐ **Jacobin Cuckoo** L: 33 cm (13")

A handsome, crested cuckoo that is mostly black and always shows a white wing patch. Two colour morphs occur in Kruger: pied and dark. The pied morph is by far the most common, and is black with plain greyish-white from vent to throat; dark-morph birds, which are very rare in the park, are all-dark apart from white wing patches and tail tips. Pied-morph Levaillant's Cuckoo is similar to pied-morph Jacobin Cuckoo but is much larger and has a longer, floppier crest and heavily streaked throat. Dark-morph Levaillant's Cuckoo is unknown from Kruger. The Jacobin Cuckoo is a fairly common spring and summer (October–April) breeding migrant to Kruger from farther north in Africa, although at the same time a few non-breeders migrate from Asia. It calls a loud *"klleeuuw-klew-klew"* and down-slurred *"klew"*. This cuckoo mostly parasitizes bulbuls and greenbuls.

PIED MORPH

☐ Black Cuckoo

L: 30 cm (12")

This large cuckoo is entirely black except for white tips to the long tail, and sometimes has white bars on the vent, tail and underside of the flight feathers. It has a characteristic swerving flight. Dark-morph Jacobin and Levaillant's Cuckoos are similar, but have crests and prominent white flashes in the wings. Black Cuckoo is an uncommon and widespread spring and summer visitor (September–March) to Kruger, preferring dense woodland and forest. It gives a mournful three-note song, *"I'm so saaaaad"*, the last note rising, sometimes followed by a rising crescendo of whistles. This cuckoo parasitizes boubous and bush-shrikes.

☐ Levaillant's Cuckoo

L: 40 cm (16")

A large, dark-backed cuckoo, with a long, floppy crest, white wing patches, and pale underparts with heavily streaked throat and lower flanks. A dark morph occurs elsewhere in Africa but is not known from Kruger. The similar but smaller Jacobin Cuckoo lacks throat streaking. Levaillant's Cuckoo is a fairly common spring and summer (October–March) breeding migrant to Kruger, where it parasitizes Arrow-marked Babblers (*page 124*). Its call is a shrill *"kreeeuu"*, often followed by chattering notes.

89

Small cuckoos with glossy green (males) or bronzy-green (females) uppersides.

☐ Diederik Cuckoo L: 19 cm (7·5")

This small 'green' cuckoo is similar to Klaas's Cuckoo and told by the pattern of green and white. The male has white underparts with barred flanks, and iridescent green upperparts with strong white flecking on the wing, white patches in front of and behind the eye, and a prominent red eye-ring and eye. The bronzy-green female has a diagnostic white patch in front of the eye and white patches on the wings. It is a common spring and summer (September–April) intra-African breeding migrant to Kruger. Although found in many habitat types, it prefers riverine and wetland areas where its preferred hosts, weavers and bishops, are common. The call is a loud, rising *"deee-deee-deee-deee-dederik"* – hence its name.

MALE

FEMALE

Klaas's Cuckoo L: 18 cm (7")

A small 'green' cuckoo. The male has white underparts and glossy, dark green upperparts, including 'spurs' that extend from the head onto the lower throat, and a conspicuous white patch behind the eye. The female is barred green-bronze on the back and head, with brown- and white-barred underparts. Both sexes lack the white flecks on the wing and in front of the eye shown by Diederik Cuckoo. Klaas's Cuckoo is an uncommon spring and summer (September–April) intra-African breeding migrant to Kruger, although some overwinter. It is much more conspicuous when calling between September and Februrary. The call is a plaintive *"meeee-jtie, meeee-tjie"*, which gives the bird its name in Afrikaans. This cuckoo feeds particularly on caterpillars and larvae, and parasitizes batises, small warblers and sunbirds.

FEMALE

MALE

☐ **Red-faced Mousebird** L: 34 cm (13")

A slaty-grey, rather rotund, long-tailed mousebird with a naked red facial patch and red feet. The tail is sleeker and longer than that of Speckled Mousebird, giving it a more streamlined flight. There is also a pale patch on the rump which can be seen as a bird flies away. This species is common and widespread in Kruger, although seemingly less abundant than Speckled Mousebird. It is somewhat nomadic, preferring woodlands and camps with suitable fruit and nectar; flowering aloes are especially favoured. In flight it gives a distinctive high-pitched *"ti-wii-wii"* call.

☐ Speckled Mousebird L: 32 cm (13")

From a distance, a brownish-grey, dumpy-bodied, short-legged bird with a long, scruffy tail. Close views reveal a buff belly, blackish face and ashy crest, and a very small bill. This mousebird is often seen creeping and scrambling through bushes and tangles, hanging on its short legs. In flight, it flutters almost desperately but quite fast, with its tail seeming to drag it down, as if it were too heavy to make it to the next bush. Small groups of these social birds are common throughout Kruger, feeding on fruit, leaves, flowers and nectar. They are sometimes seen hanging upside-down by their dull purplish feet, exposing the black skin on their bellies to absorb heat: this aids digestion and helps the birds to warm up on cool mornings. Speckled Mousebirds breed co-operatively, with youngsters from the previous year helping their parents raise a new brood, and will huddle together in small groups to stay warm when roosting.

☐ **Striped Kingfisher** L: 18 cm (7")

A small and dainty woodland-dwelling kingfisher, less dramatically blue and grey than the larger species, with powder-blue tail and flight feathers, mouse-brown back, creamy collar, dark eyestripe and a streaky brown crown. The bicoloured bill is brown above and orange below. This widespread and fairly common resident is inconspicuous unless it is singing its loud, ringing, territorial *"teeep-tiiiirrrrrrr"*, or rollicking *"trrreerrr-treeerr-treeer"* songs. It favours open parkland, avoiding dense woodland and forest and feeds mainly on small insects. Birds will chase larger competitors, such as shrikes and rollers, and may even try to see off humans in their territory. When an aerial predator is seen, this kingfisher freezes, bill pointed skywards, and turns its body slowly to keep the predator in view.

☐ **Woodland Kingfisher**
L: 23 cm (9")

A thickset kingfisher – electric blue on the back, with a diagnostic red-and-black bill. The head and breast are blue-grey, and there are dark panels on the shoulders and wingtips. This is a common breeding migrant (November–April) to Kruger from farther north in Africa, and its loud and characteristic song, a high-pitched *"tuuui"*, followed by a pause and a trilling, down-slurred *"trrrrrrrrrrrrrrrrrr"*, heralds the beginning of the rainy season. Birds sometimes advertise their presence by sitting bolt upright, extending their wings to show a bold wing pattern, and calling loudly. The Woodland Kingfisher is not at all tied to water, feeding on invertebrates and small vertebrates in woodland, including around many camps.

Brown-hooded Kingfisher
L: 21 cm (8")

This kingfisher has a blue tail
and flight feathers, dark brown
back and shoulders, a dull,
grey-brown streaked head,
dark-tipped reddish bill and
red legs. The similar Grey-headed
Kingfisher has a chestnut belly
and a 'cleaner' look to the head.
The Brown-hooded Kingfisher
is a common resident in Kruger,
favouring thicker habitat than
Woodland Kingfisher where it feeds
on insects and small vertebrates.
The song is a soft, short, descending
"ki-ti-ti-ti-it".

Grey-headed Kingfisher
L: 21 cm (8")

A kingfisher with a sapphire-blue
tail and flight feathers, dark brown
back, clear ashy-grey head and
breast, chestnut belly and
vermilion bill. It is a widespread
but uncommon spring and summer
(September–May) breeding migrant
to Kruger, although less numerous in
drier years. This kingfisher prefers lush
savannah near water. It excavates its
nesting burrows mainly in riverbanks,
although has been known to use old
aardvark burrows. For a kingfisher,
the song is weak and unobtrusive: a
trilling "t-t-t-t-t-t-t" and a repeated
squeaky "tsury, tsury".

Bee-eaters are slender, long-tailed birds that feed in the air, gliding between deep, quick beats of long, pointed wings.

SOUTHERN CARMINE BEE-EATER

☐ European Bee-eater L: 25–28 cm (10–11")

This is a large, strikingly coloured bee-eater with a chestnut-and-golden back, turquoise blue underparts, and a canary-yellow throat. Females and juveniles are duller than males, and juveniles lack the adults' pointed central tail feathers. Although small numbers can occur year-round, it is a common and widespread spring and summer visitor (October–April) to Kruger, where it can aggregate in huge numbers. Flocks passing overhead are often detected by delicate and fluid "*pruuip*" and "*kwip-kwip*" flight calls. Bee-eaters are agile, adept fliers, either hawking insects in the air, or from a regular perch to which they return and where prey is bludgeoned before being swallowed.

EUROPEAN BEE-EATER

Southern Carmine Bee-eater L: 38 cm (15")

IMMATURE

A large, spectacular, long, slender, carmine-pink and teal-blue bee-eater with a long, pointed tail and black bill and facial mask. Immatures are duller than adults and lack long tail feathers. It is a common non-breeding summer migrant (December–April) to Kruger, where it can gather in large groups and often attends bush fires to feed on fleeing insects. The *"trik-trik-trik"* or *"ga-ga-ga"* calls, sound more guttural than those of European Bee-eater. Although not a common behaviour, Southern Carmine Bee-eaters have been recorded sitting on the backs of antelopes or Kori Bustards (*page 66*), swooping out and catching insects that are flushed. It specializes in catching large flying insects, including termites, cicadas, dragonflies, butterflies and locusts and regurgitates pellets of indigestible insect remains.

☐ White-fronted Bee-eater L: 23 cm (9")

This bee-eater's bright and distinctive colours and pattern make it unmistakable: look for the white face, bold black mask, red throat and square green tail. It is a common resident that is almost always found close to the sandy banks of larger rivers, where it breeds. It has a complex social system, with the dominant breeding pair assisted by several helpers to form families, and families banding together to form clans, which defend feeding territories from other clans. Some 'pirates' may remain at the breeding colony, waiting for unrelated birds to return with food, which they steal and feed to their own chicks! In addition, some females lay eggs in the nests of unwary neighbours; literally dumping the burden of raising their chicks into another pair's nest, like a cuckoo. Colonies are often raided by monitor lizards and egg-eating snakes.

☐ Little Bee-eater L: 15 cm (6")

A tiny, colourful, mostly grass-green bee-eater with a canary-yellow throat separated from burnt-cinnamon underparts by a black gorget. It has rufous wings and a black-tipped tail but these are obvious only in flight. This is an uncommon resident throughout Kruger, with small parties darting around clearings, calling a sibilant "*s-lip*" and other high-pitched notes. Birds often perch relatively inconspicuously on small twigs and branches, often lower than 1·5 m above the ground, from which they make sallies to catch insects. At night, small parties may roost shoulder-to-shoulder to stay warm.

☐ Broad-billed Roller L: 30 cm (12")

A medium-sized, dark, rufous-cinnamon bird with a short, broad and chunky yellow bill. In flight it is shaped much like a small, thickset falcon, but has deep wing beats and an undulating flight action. It is an uncommon spring and summer visitor (September–April) to Kruger, particularly north of Shingwedzi, where it breeds in riverine forest and lush savannah. The calls are scratchy *"grrrrrr"* and *"k-weeek, k-weeek"* notes, higher pitched, less varied, and less harsh than those of other rollers. Compared to other rollers (*pages 100–101*) this species tends to forage higher in the air, and also perches higher, often on bare snags in and above the canopy.

☐ Lilac-breasted Roller L: 36 cm (14")

An eyecatching, chunky, large-headed bird with a pastel lilac breast, rosy cheeks and a pale green crown. Although it has a longer tail than the European Roller, and appears slimmer, the breast colour is the most striking difference. The Lilac-breasted Roller is a common resident throughout Kruger, selecting conspicuous perches from which to search for prey, mostly insects and small vertebrates. It is usually silent, but sometimes calls a loud, guttural *"gwhaaak, gwhaaak"*. This species has an amazing display flight that includes the side-to-side rolling that gives this group of birds their name. In flight, it shows four electric shades of blue in the wings and in good light is certainly breathtaking; this is the bird that most frequently gets dedicated mammal-watchers and photographers into birding!

PURPLE ROLLER

EUROPEAN ROLLER

UPPERWING

LILAC-BREASTED ROLLER

UNDERWING

☐ Purple Roller

L: 35–40 cm (14–16")

The bulkiest and dullest of the rollers, with primarily purple-cinnamon hues flecked with many fine white streaks and a bold white eyebrow. In flight, however, it shows purple-blue on the wings, tail and vent. The bill is dark, separating it from the smaller and scarcer Broad-billed Roller (*page 99*). The Purple Roller is an uncommon resident in Kruger, generally preferring drier woodland compared with other rollers. Aerial displays include side-to-side rolling while giving loud, guttural *"ghaaaa"* calls.

NT ☐ European Roller

L: 30 cm (12")

This powerful, bulky roller is mostly a pale greenish sky-blue, with a brown back, and has a short, square tail lacking a central spike. In flight, it shows striking ultramarine underwings and shoulder patches. It is an abundant non-breeding summer visitor (November–March), when it is the most common roller in Kruger, often being seen perched up on snags watching for large insect prey. Although birds can give a harsh croak, this roller is mostly silent in South Africa.

☐ Green Woodhoopoe
L: 37 cm (15")

An elongated, metallic green-black bird
with a long, downcurved, red-orange bill,
red legs and a long, floppy, white-tipped
tail. Juveniles have dark bills and resemble
Common Scimitarbill, but are larger and
normally accompanied by adults. It is
a common resident in Kruger, where it
is frequently seen in camps, clinging to
trees and stumps, and flying clumsily with
tail dangling. It is a highly social species,
communicating by a loud, cackling, almost
maniacal, chatter. Small parties clamber in
trees, probing bark and crevices for insects,
spiders and small vertebrates. An alpha
female dominates each group, and alpha
pairs are highly faithful, with a less than
1% 'divorce' rate. The remainder of the
group helps the pair raise their offspring
and defends the territory co-operatively.
Woodhoopoes nest and roost in holes,
where they are vulnerable to predation
by genets, African Harrier-Hawk (*page
201*) and snakes. Greater and Lesser
Honeyguides (*page 110*) are known to be
brood parasites of this bird.

JUVENILE

Common Scimitarbill L: 30 cm (12")

Similar to the Green Woodhoopoe but
smaller and daintier, lacking a greenish
gloss, and with a slender and more strongly
downcurved black bill and black legs.
Females and juveniles are browner on the
head than males, and their bills are shorter
and less downcurved. This species is fairly
common throughout Kruger, but is less
conspicuous than the Green Woodhoopoe.
It is most easily detected by its plaintive,
high-pitched, three-note whistled *"wheeep,
wheeep, wheeep"* song, and *"ker-ker-ker"*
calls. Birds forage by clambering around
on trunks, probing for invertebrates,
and will often join mixed-species flocks.
Competition for food between the sexes
may be reduced as a result of their slightly
different bill shapes and foraging strategies:
males concentrate on larger branches and
females on smaller ones. Unlike the Green
Woodhoopoe, the Common Scimitarbill is
not a co-operative breeder.

The preen glands of woodhoopoes and
scimitarbills produce a foul-smelling
secretion which acts as an effective
predator deterrent.

Hornbills are medium to large birds with large, slightly downcurved bills. They have a bizarre breeding system: the female is sealed into a cavity by her mate, lays 3–5 eggs and undergoes a full moult, rendering her flightless and helpless. During this time the male provisions the entire family through a narrow slit opening: the female breaks out post-moult, when she and the young are ready to fly.

Red-billed Hornbill L: 35–45 cm (14–18")

This small, black-and-white hornbill is readily identified by its relatively small red bill, males having a black base to the lower mandible. The similar Southern Yellow-billed Hornbill is larger, with a robust yellow bill, and the rarer Crowned Hornbill (not illustrated) has a uniform brown back and orange bill. The Red-billed Hornbill is a very common resident in open woodland throughout Kruger. Its territorial display, with head bowed and wings spread, starts with a series of "*kok-kok-kok*" calls, followed by two-syllable "*kokok-kokok*" notes. This is one of the most terrestrial hornbills, with prey usually taken on the ground; this may explain the birds' preference for open areas that have been heavily trampled by ungulates and elephants.

MALE

FEMALE

☐ Southern Yellow-billed Hornbill

L: 48–60 cm (19–24")

A medium-sized, mostly black-and-white
hornbill with white-spotted shoulders,
pinkish-red facial skin and a diagnostic
yellow bill that gives it the local Kruger
nickname of 'flying banana'. It is a very
common resident in Kruger, and one
of the most conspicuous picnic site and
camp birds, where it waits for hand
outs and searches for scraps. The most
frequent territorial display is a continuous
rollicking set of *"ko-ko, ko-ko"* notes,
working up to a crescendo *"ko-kukuk,
ko-kukuk, ko-kukuk"* with wings open and
head bowed.

☐ African Grey Hornbill L: 43–48 cm (17–19")

A medium-sized, ashy-coloured hornbill with
pale-edged back feathers, a creamy belly and a
long, pale eyebrow. The curved, tapered bill differs
between the sexes: males have a mostly dark bill
with a pale wedge at the base and a larger casque;
the female's bill is mostly ivory above with a
purple-reddish tip. This hornbill has a buoyant and
undulating flight, when it can be readily identified
by its pale rump and tail tips. It is a common
resident in woodland throughout Kruger. To
proclaim their territory, birds give a long series of
plaintive, piping *"piu-piu-piu"* notes that conclude
with some rolling whistles, with the bill raised
skywards and the wings flicked with each note.

The Zulus believe that the hornbill is an eternal
optimist, always looking up to the heavens and
hoping for a better future even in the fiercest drought.
They therefore call it umkolwana – the 'believer'.

SOUTHERN GROUND–HORNBILL

AFRICAN GREY HORNBILL

MALE

FEMALE

EN ☐ **Southern Ground-Hornbill** L: 90–130 cm (35–51")

One of the BIG 6

This enormous, gregarious, terrestrial hornbill is easily recognised. It is black, with white wingtips that are obvious only in flight. The male has a brilliant red face and throat wattles; the female is similar but has purple-blue skin in the centre of the throat patch; immatures are scruffy, with yellowish facial skin. The number of birds in Kruger is estimated to be 600–700 individuals, and more than 40 nests have been located; this represents about 35% of the population in the whole of South Africa. Groups have territory sizes of up to 100 km². In the early morning, dominant pairs indulge in some deep bass duet booming, which can be heard several kilometres away. Despite its relative scarcity, this bird is very conspicuous and small groups are frequently seen walking slowly through bushy savannah searching for invertebrate prey. They can be incredibly tame, sometimes causing traffic jams because of their unwillingness to yield to cars! These birds indulge in some strange breeding behaviour. Within a group, only the dominant pair breeds, and they are very choosy about their nest site, selecting a perfect-sized cavity in a large fig or other suitable tree. This pair is assisted by between 1–9 helpers, usually male birds from previous broods. Sealed into the nest cavity, the female incubates the eggs, relying on the male and helpers to supply her with food. The first hatched chick dominates its younger siblings, which normally starve, leaving just one survivor. This behaviour also occurs in certain raptors, where the second chick is solely for insurance in case the first perishes. These birds are extremely long-lived, up to 30–40 years, and given their slow reproduction rate, are the terrestrial equivalents of albatrosses when it comes to life history strategies.

Smallish, thickset, short-legged, large-headed birds with a stout bill; most are boldly patterned and have distinctive calls. They nest in tree holes.

☐ Yellow-fronted Tinkerbird

L: 12 cm (4·5")

Tinkerbirds are tiny, woodland barbets. This species is told by its yellow-orange forehead patch and prominently white-speckled black shoulders and back of the head. The similar Yellow-rumped Tinkerbird (not illustrated), which is rare in Kruger, lacks a forehead patch. The Yellow-fronted Tinkerbird is locally uncommon north of the Levuvu River and also around Pretoriuskop in the southwest of the park; it is rare elsewhere. The repetitive *"pok-pok-pok"* call can last for minutes, and is often the first sign that the bird is present. It favours the fruits of mistletoe and figs, and is an important dispersal agent of these plants.

☐ Crested Barbet L: 23 cm (9")

This thickset, pale-billed, crested, fiery-coloured barbet is a common, widespread and conspicuous resident bird in Kruger's woodlands. It gives an incessant unmusical dry trill, rising towards the end – like a broken ticker-tape machine. Pairs have a strong bond, and duetting throughout the year helps to strengthen their relationship. It is the most terrestrial of the barbets, frequently hopping on the ground to feed on insects, although it also takes fruits.

☐ **Black-collared Barbet** L: 20 cm (8")

A chunky, bulky-headed barbet with a pale lemon-yellow belly and a black hood and collar splashed with irregularly edged vivid scarlet on the face and breast. It is a common resident throughout Kruger, including in most of the camps. It sings a characteristic duet *"two-pudley, two-pudley, two-pudley"* that can go on for a minute or more. The preferred food is the fruits of figs and waterberries, although it will eat other fruits and insects, especially when feeding chicks. This barbet is a co-operative breeder, with helpers assisting with nest excavation, defence, incubation and feeding chicks. They either excavate their own hole or commandeer the nest of woodpeckers or glossy-starlings.

Honeyguides are true oddities. Some species guide both humans and Honey Badgers to bees' nests, where they expect their followers to take the honey, leaving the eggs, larvae and wax to the honeyguide. This behaviour seems to be genetically determined. There are many folk tales of spurned honeyguides exacting revenge by leading people to dangerous animals, but this is neither proven nor likely. Honeyguides, like cuckoos, are brood parasites and exploit hole-nesters such as woodpeckers and barbets to raise their chicks. Honeyguides chicks have hook-tipped bills, and upon hatching will maul or eject any host chicks in the nest to improve their own chances of survival.

☐ Lesser Honeyguide L: 14 cm (5·5")

The Lesser Honeyguide is similar to the Greater Honeyguide in overall shape and in having bold white outer tail feathers, but is much smaller. It also has a chunkier bill with a small white spot at the base, a slate-grey head with black moustachial streaks, and an olive-green back (in contrast to the Greater Honeyguide which has a plain brownish crown and back). Lesser Honeyguide is an uncommon and unobtrusive bird throughout Kruger and, like the Greater Honeyguide, is most often seen in flight. The call is a continuous series of strident *"swiiit, swiiit, swiiit"* notes. This species is not known to guide, but still feeds on beeswax, bees and other insects.

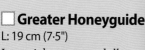 Greater Honeyguide

L: 19 cm (7·5")

Its upright posture, dull grey-brown coloration, and conspicuous white outer feathers to the short tail identify this bird as a honeyguide. The Greater Honeyguide can be distinguished by an unmarked grey-brown back and crown, with frosted white edgings to the shoulder feathers. The sexes differ: males have a distinctive pink bill, black throat and large white 'ear-muffs'; females have a black bill and pale throat. Immatures are also distinctive, having a yellow throat and breast. The smaller Lesser Honeyguide has a streaky green back and wings, and all-grey (not brown) head. Greater Honeyguide is a widespread but uncommon and inconspicuous bird in Kruger, most often seen in undulating flight or tracked down by a series of strident two-note "*VIC-tor, VIC-tor, VIC-tor*" vocalizations.

FEMALE

MALE

Woodpeckers have stiff spine-like tail feathers to provide support when perched on a tree trunk, and unusual feet, with two toes pointing forwards and two pointing backwards, to give a firm grip. An extremely long, barbed tongue and sticky saliva help to capture pupae, larvae and insects exposed when probing wood and bark.

☐ Bearded Woodpecker L: 25 cm (10")

A large, long-billed woodpecker with a brown back, barred belly, and strong black pattern on the head; the crown is black in the female and red and black in the male. Although widespread and resident throughout Kruger's lush savannah it is more solitary and less frequently encountered than other woodpeckers. It gives sharp *"kwip-kwip-kwip"* calls, and has a characteristic 'drum' that lasts about five seconds, beginning fast and then slowing.

FEMALE

MALE

☐ Bennett's Woodpecker L: 23 cm (9")

This medium-sized woodpecker is the only one in Kruger with spotted rather than streaked or barred underparts. It is pale beneath, and green with white spots above. It is a fairly common breeding resident throughout Kruger, preferring mature broadleaved woodland and avoiding drier scrub. Ants, termites and larvae form the bulk of the diet.

Key features to look for when identifying a woodpecker are whether the breast is streaked, spotted or barred, and the facial pattern.

FEMALE

MALE

MALE

FEMALE

☐ **Golden-tailed Woodpecker** L: 21 cm (8")

Most of Kruger's woodpeckers have 'golden' tails, so this is a poor identification feature. The Golden-tailed Woodpecker is a mid-sized woodpecker with a streaky breast and throat. In comparison, the rarer Bennett's Woodpecker (*page 113*) has spotted (not streaked) underparts, and the much smaller Cardinal Woodpecker has a solid black moustachial streak. Golden-tailed Woodpecker is a common resident throughout Kruger's woodlands, where it joins flocks and excavates tree bark for insects. A strange shrieking *"wheeaa-aaaa"* call often betrays its presence.

☐ Cardinal Woodpecker

L: 15 cm (6")

A small, compact woodpecker, with heavily streaked underparts and a solid black moustachial streak. The nape is red in the male and black in the female. The larger Golden-tailed and Bennett's Woodpeckers (*page 113*) have more red on the crown, and longer bills. It is common throughout Kruger's woodlands where its trilled rattle call reveals its presence as it forages, either alone or in flocks of other birds, along small dead branches and twigs that are ignored by larger woodpeckers.

Woodpeckers have several adaptations that allow them to be masters of their environment. They have strong bills and modified brain cavities that have evolved to be able to absorb the mechanical stress of vigorous pecking and drumming. Woodpeckers also have long, sticky and barbed tongues that help them to extract their prey. Most importantly, they have strong and barbed tail feathers which act as a prop when they are perched, and modified feet with two toes pointing forwards and two pointing backwards (an unusual arrangement called zygodactyly), which helps the bird to remain stable when foraging, and to climb vertically up tree trunks.

FEMALE

MALE

These unrelated but similar-looking species are frequently found in mixed species flocks, and can therefore easily be confused.

☐ Southern Black Tit L: 15 cm (6")

A small, active and noisy black bird, with a short bill, white shoulders and white edgings to its wing feathers. It is a common resident in Kruger, particularly in broadleaved woodland, where it is a core species in mixed feeding flocks. This bird is often detected by its noisy buzzing and chirping vocalizations, including a characteristic *"diddy-dzee-dzee-dzee-dzee-dzee"*. It is a co-operative breeder that will nest in abandoned barbet and woodpecker holes.

☐ Southern Black Flycatcher
L: 18 cm (7")

An upright, slim, and lustrous all-black bird, with dark-brown eyes and straight-edged, square or minutely notched tail; juveniles are spotted brown. Drongos differ by having red eyes and broad, forked tails; the male Black Cuckooshrike has an orange base to the bill and creeps and hops horizontally through trees. The Southern Black Flycatcher is a common and widespread resident in Kruger's woodlands and camps, but more secretive than drongos, often perching in the mid-storey. It is mostly silent, but sometimes sings a three-note *"tseeep-tsoo-tsoo"* song.

☐ Black Cuckooshrike L: 20 cm (8")

The sexes of the Black Cuckooshrike are very different: the male is a dumpy, all-black bird with a yellow-orange base to the gape and a usually inconspicuous yellow shoulder mark; the female is a more distinctive grey-brown with bars below and bright yellow edges to the wing and tail feathers. The male could be confused with a Fork-tailed Drongo or Southern Black Flycatcher, but can be told by its more horizontal posture and sluggish behaviour; the drongo also has pale wing feathers in flight. This is an uncommon and unobtrusive resident of Kruger, its presence often revealed by a prolonged insect-like *"trrrrrrrrr"* trill. It may join flocks of other birds, but can also be solitary, searching the canopy for caterpillars and other arboreal prey.

☐ Fork-tailed Drongo L: 25 cm (10")

This black, red-eyed, upright bird has a long narrow tail that splays out into a wide fork at the tip. In flight, a useful identification feature is the paler flight feathers. Abundant and conspicuous throughout Kruger, it prefers open wooded country. It sings a varied series of unmelodic, noisy and mechanical notes, sometimes including mimicry. Drongos hawk insects from a perch, and can associate with ungulates, catching insects that they flush. They will also associate with foraging mongooses, giving false alarm calls to distract their attention before stealing their hard-earned pickings.

MALE   FEMALE

A mixed assemblage of birds from various families that are most frequently encountered in the well-watered gardens of Kruger's camps.

☐ Dark-capped Bulbul L: 18 cm (7")

Bulbuls are upright birds with slight crests, rather stout bills and loud, musical songs. Greenbuls and brownbuls (see *page 170*) are members of the same family but are generally larger and less conspicuous. This slender, grey-brown bird with a pale belly, conspicuous yellow vent, black face, and a scruffy crest is an abundant resident in Kruger, and one of the commonest birds across much of Africa. From dawn till dusk they can be seen, sometimes in small groups, giving a loud, cheerful variable *"quick-chop-toquick"* song. The Dark-capped Bulbul is highly vigilant and is often the first species to find snakes, owls or similar dangers, attracting other mobbing birds with a loud nasal *"kik-kik-kik"* alarm call. It feeds primarily on fruits but may also take invertebrates.

☐ Black-headed Oriole L: 20–24 cm (8–9")

Despite their bright plumage, orioles have an amazing ability to hide away in dense foliage. This spectacular, mostly golden-yellow bird has a black head and pink-orange bill; the wings and tail have splashes of black and white; juveniles have a dirty olive-brown hood and bill. This common Kruger resident is conspicuous in camps, where it feeds on insects, fruit and nectar, often drawing attention with a musical and liquid *"wholeuooo"* call.

☐ Kurrichane Thrush L: 21 cm (8")

Thrushes are long-tailed, rounded, large-headed birds that often sing from elevated perches and hop, run or shuffle on the ground when feeding. The Kurrichane Thrush is grey-olive with a white belly and buff flanks. Adults have a distinctive bright orange bill and eye-ring, and a pale throat with broad black moustachial streaks; juveniles have black-spotted underparts and a dusky-orange bill. This is a common and widespread resident in Kruger, inhabiting open woodlands, including camps, where it runs on the ground, foraging for mainly invertebrate food. It sings a series of varied fluted notes and whistles, and is known to mimic the sounds of other birds.

DARK-CAPPED BULBUL

BLACK-HEADED ORIOLE

Sparrows are small, weaver-like, stout-billed birds.

☐ Southern Grey-headed Sparrow L: 15 cm (6")

This sparrow has a plain grey head and underparts, and a brown rump, mantle and wings, with a variable (sometimes absent) white wingbar below the shoulders. The stout bill is black in the breeding season, but otherwise horn-coloured. It is a common resident throughout Kruger, equally happy in natural woodland and near human habitation, feeding on seeds, insects, and human discards. The calls are a series of simple, repetitive chipping notes. It nests in a variety of cavities, including in buildings and disused swallow nests, and is parasitized by Diederik Cuckoo (*page 90*).

☐ House Sparrow L: 15 cm (6")

The male House Sparrow has a black bib, a grey crown with brown sides, streaky chestnut-and-brown back and wings, and a prominent white fleck on the shoulder. Females and juveniles are much drabber: brown and grey with a streaky back, shoulders and wings. Both sexes are unstreaked grey below. The House Sparrow is a common resident throughout Kruger, especially close to humans, including in camps and picnic areas. It gives an incessant "*chirrup*" call that will be familiar to most of the world's city residents. It feeds on seeds, invertebrates and nectar, but is also one of the primary beneficiaries of human-created waste and food.

☐ Cape White-eye L: 12 cm (4.5")

This small, active, yellow-green, warbler-like bird has an obvious white eye-ring. In most of Kruger it is unmistakable, but along the Levuvu and Limpopo rivers in the far north, it overlaps with the very similar, but much rarer, Yellow White-eye (not illustrated). As its name suggests, the Yellow White-eye differs by having more intense yellow underparts and a yellow forehead. The Cape White-eye is a very common resident throughout Kruger, where it occurs in most habitats in single-species or mixed foraging flocks feeding on nectar, fruits and small invertebrates. A sweet, rolling, reedy warble is often the first sign of its presence.

SOUTHERN GREY-HEADED SPARROW

HOUSE SPARROW

MALE

FEMALE

☐ Groundscraper Thrush L: 21 cm (8")

A tall, long-legged thrush with grey-brown upperparts, heavily streaked white underparts, and a strongly marked face with a bold black moustache, tear-stripe, and ear-crescent on an otherwise white face. In flight it shows distinctive large buff patches in the wings. This is a common resident of open woodlands and camps throughout Kruger, favouring heavily grazed and burnt areas. Numbers may decline in winter (June–August), and although locally nomadic movements sometimes occur, these are poorly understood. The Groundscraper Thrush sings a melodic song, and calls a grating *"lit-sit-siru-pa"* (which gives the bird its scientific name *Psophocichla litsitsirupa*). It runs long distances on the ground before stopping and standing bolt-upright and flicking its wings.

☐ Bushveld Pipit L: 13 cm (5")

Pipits are more slender and thinner-billed than larks, and this species is smaller and dumpier than the other pipits in Kruger. Its streaky back and breast prevent confusion with the scarce and erratic Buffy and Plain-backed Pipits (neither illustrated), and compared with African Pipit (*page 73*) the streaking is more extensive on the breast, reaching the flanks. Bushveld Pipit also lacks the bold white eyebrow of African Pipit and has a shorter tail. It is an uncommon and unobtrusive resident in Kruger that is somewhat nomadic, favouring the western woodlands in the southern half of the park. It avoids open areas and stubble fields (favoured by African Pipit), preferring the undergrowth of woodland, particularly where it is grassy or rocky.

☐ Sabota Lark L: 15 cm (6")

A medium-sized, streaky lark with a conspicuous white eyebrow, white crescent under the eye and prominent moustachial streak, creating a bold face pattern. The breast is strongly streaked, contrasting with a whitish belly and throat. This species lacks the rufous in the wing shown by Rufous-naped Lark (*page 73*) and Flappet Lark (not illustrated). It is a common resident in Kruger, where pairs inhabit a variety of drier woodlands. In spring and summer (October–March), birds sit up on thorn trees singing a rich melodious and variable song that often includes mimicry of other birds.

GROUNDSCRAPER THRUSH

BUSHVELD PIPIT

☐ White-browed Scrub-Robin L: 15 cm (6")

Scrub-robins are like small thrushes in shape and behaviour. This species has grey-brown upperparts, two diagnostic white wingbars, pale streaked underparts and a prominent white eyebrow and moustache. A rufous rump and sides to the tail, and dark bar and white tips give the tail a distinctive appearance, especially when the bird is flying away. This is a very common resident in drier woodland and scrub in Kruger, often seen running on the ground and lifting its tail. Although it may skulk in dense vegetation, it sometimes perches in a prominent position singing its characteristic *"twee-too-too"* song, or a variation of other quavering sweet notes.

☐ Arrow-marked Babbler L: 23 cm (9")

Babblers are gregarious, grey-brown birds of low bushes. The Arrow-marked Babbler has striking yellow-and-red eyes, and a multitude of tiny white chevrons on the head and breast that give the bird its name. This is a common resident throughout Kruger, preferring dry woodland and riverine thickets where it occurs in single-species or mixed flocks; it is frequently seen in camps. A dry, gurgling babble *"gra-gra-gra-gra-gra"* is made by several birds in a group. Each group defends a large territory, the birds foraging for insects, spiders and small vertebrates on the ground or in low shrubs and trees, and co-operatively raises the chicks of the dominant pair. The Arrow-marked Babbler is the main host species for the parasitic Levaillant's Cuckoo (*page 89*).

Mocking Cliff-Chat L: 22 cm (9")

The sexes of this long-tailed, strong-legged ground bird look very different. The stunning male has glossy black upperparts, chestnut underparts and rump, and a bold white shoulder patch; the female is duller, with slaty grey-brown upperparts, deeper rufous underparts, and lacks the white shoulder patch. This bird has a distinctive habit of slowly lifting its tail when perched. It is a fairly common resident in Kruger, but restricted to rocky outcrops and boulder-strewn woodland. It is often detected by its loud, complex, melodic song, sometimes given in duet, and often including mimicry.

MALE

MOCKING CLIFF-CHAT

FEMALE

ARROW-MARKED BABBLER

☐ Yellow-breasted Apalis L: 12 cm (4·5")

This small, long-tailed, canopy-dwelling, warbler-like
bird has green upperparts, a grey head with a striking
red eye, and a yellow breast and white belly separated by
a variable black bar (sometimes lacking in the female). It
is a common resident in mixed woodlands throughout
Kruger, where it may be seen feeding actively in the
canopy of thorn trees, sometimes in mixed-species
flocks, flicking its tail as it moves. However, it is most
often detected by its repeated, grating *"chrr-eek-chrr-eek-
chrr-eek"* territorial call given in duet by both sexes.

☐ Long-billed Crombec L: 11 cm (4·5")

Crombecs are tiny, rotund and virtually tailless warbler-like birds, usually first recognised
by their shape. The Long-billed Crombec has buff-orange underparts, an indistinct
eyebrow, grey-brown upperparts, and a fairly long, dark, downcurved bill. It is a common
resident throughout Kruger, where it may be seen singly or in mixed-species flocks
hopping actively along branches, and occasionally hanging underneath like a nuthatch,
searching for its mainly invertebrate food. It has a quiet but distinctive faltering *"chirrit,
chirrit, chirrit"* song, and quavering *"prrrp"* call.

☐ Willow Warbler L: 12 cm (4·5")

The Old World warblers are mostly small, slim, thin-billed birds, favouring either
the foliage of trees and bushes or wetland habitats. The Willow Warbler is a small,
nondescript olive-green warbler with off-white underparts, a conspicuous pale eyebrow
that extends behind the eye, and pinkish-brown legs. The similar but uncommon Icterine
Warbler (not illustrated) is bulkier, has a broader, spike-like bill, lacks the distinct eyebrow
and has lead-grey legs (it also lacks a dark stripe in front of the eye usually shown by
Willow Warbler). The Willow Warbler's habitat choice of woodlands and gardens, and its
lively and restless demeanour, eliminate many look-alike species. Although this spring
and summer (September–April) visitor from Eurasia is common to abundant throughout
Kruger, it can be easily overlooked due to its small size and unobtrusive nature. A simple
"hoo-eet" contact call is often the first clue to its presence.

YELLOW-BREASTED APALIS

LONG-BILLED CROMBEC

WILLOW WARBLER

These unrelated species are typically found in savannah dominated by thorn trees.

☐ Chinspot Batis L: 13 cm (5")

A small, big-headed, neatly patterned grey, black and white flycatcher-like bird with yellow eyes. The sexes look quite different: the male has a broad black chest-band and a white throat; the female has a chestnut chest-band and large chestnut throat spot, which gives the species its name. The Cape Batis (not illustrated), which is a rare visitor to Kruger, differs in having reddish eyes and deep rufous flanks and wing-bands in both sexes. The Chinspot Batis is a common resident in woodland, where it can be found in pairs or mixed-species flocks, flitting actively from tree to tree gleaning and hawking insects. It has a characteristic descending three-note whistled song, *"three-blind-mice"*, which is occasionally accompanied by clicking and bill snapping.

In winter and early spring, up to ten birds may gather in small single-sex groups called 'batis parliaments'. Although they call, display and fight with each other, the function of these associations is poorly understood.

MALE

FEMALE

☐ **Rattling Cisticola** L: 15 cm (6")

Cisticolas are a group of small, brown and rufous warblers that look similar but have striking and distinctive vocalizations. The Rattling Cisticola is a conspicuous and relatively chunky, long-tailed pale brown species with a rusty crown and wings, and a mottled grey-brown back. It is an abundant resident throughout Kruger's drier woodlands, where it is one of the most obvious 'LBJs' (little brown jobs). It often sits in a prominent position on a roadside bush singing its loud *"tseeew-tseeew-tseeew"* song, frequently finishing with the *"trt-trt-trt"* rattle that gives the bird its name, and will also give a loud, scolding *"cheee"* call when alarmed.

☐ **Burnt-necked Eremomela**
L: 11 cm (4·5")

Small and nondescript, this warbler has greyish upperparts, pale buff underparts and a distinctive whitish eye. Its diagnostic rusty ear-patches and small bar across the breast are difficult to see, and in winter (June–August) are often absent. In Kruger, this eremomela is fairly common in its preferred Umbrella Thorn woodland habitat, but is very unobtrusive and easily overlooked. It may join mixed-species flocks and is most often detected by its high-pitched, accelerating, trilled song.

☐ **Spotted Flycatcher** L: 14 cm (5·5")

A nondescript, slender, upright, mouse-brown flycatcher with a softly streaked crown, throat and breast, appearing pale, silky buff-white when viewed from the front. This species has longer wings and tail and a more peaked crown than the similar African Dusky Flycatcher (*page 174*) and does not have pale lores (in front of the eye). It breeds across Eurasia and is a common spring and summer visitor (October–April) to woodlands and camps in Kruger, with some individuals returning to the same woodland patch each year. It hawks for insects from a prominent perch, sometimes hovering and frequently returning to the same position. The call, a short shrill *"zee"*, is unobtrusive and heard only infrequently in South Africa.

☐ **Grey Tit-Flycatcher** L: 14 cm (5·5")

A plumbeous-grey flycatcher that has a blackish tail with white outer feathers. It forages more like a warbler than a typical flycatcher, flitting through foliage and searching the underside of leaves for insects, seldom sallying to fly-catch. Birds often lean forward in a horizontal posture with tail slightly raised and spread, exposing the bold white feathers – a behaviour that may flush insects nearby. This species has a small white eyebrow and lacks the white eye-ring of Ashy Flycatcher. It is an uncommon and widespread Kruger resident, found in thickets and woodland margins, but is unobtrusive and most easily tracked down by its trembling, mournful *"wheeely-wheerr"* song.

☐ **Ashy Flycatcher** L: 14 cm (5·5")

An upright, slim, grey flycatcher, with a white eye-ring broken by a dark stripe through the eye, and a short pale eyebrow. It lacks the white outer tail feathers and horizontal posture of the otherwise very similar Grey-Tit-Flycatcher. This is a common resident in dense woodland and riverine forest in Kruger, numbers sometimes increasing in winter (June–August) as altitudinal migrants escape the chillier climes of the mountains nearby. It hawks for insects and returns to a prominent perch, and may join mixed-species flocks. The call is a descending *"pit-pit-pit-pit…"*.

SPOTTED FLYCATCHER

GREY TIT-FLYCATCHER

Bush-shrikes are small to medium-sized, strikingly coloured and patterned birds. They tend to creep stealthily through trees and bushes, although some species are more terrestrial, and have loud, distinctive vocalizations.

☐ Black-backed Puffback L: 17 cm (6·5")

A small, canopy-loving, black-and-white bush-shrike with a fiery-red eye. The fluffy white feathers on the rump of the male can be raised like a puffball when the bird is excited. The sexes also look different: the male has a clean-cut black cap and a white throat, while the female is greyer on the head with a white forehead and partial eyebrow giving it a pale and open face. This species is a common and widespread resident throughout Kruger, with a population estimated at more than 130,000 individuals. It is found in pairs in riverine forest and woodlands and often joins mixed-species flocks. It is readily detected by its characteristic call: a loud click, followed by a repeated down-slurred "*wheeeoo*" whistle.

☐ Black-crowned Tchagra L: 21 cm (8")

Tchagras are buff-brown bush-shrikes with strong, black bills, broad rufous wing panels and white-tipped dark tails. They favour low thickets and are most often seen as they fly between bushes. The head pattern is an important feature for identifying the two species in Kruger. The Black-crowned Tchagra is the larger of the two and has an all-black cap, a bold white line above a black eyestripe, and greyish underparts contrasting with rufous wings. It is a common and widespread resident in Kruger, although it favours the more open eastern sectors of the park over the dense thickets that predominate in the west. It occurs both on the ground and in trees in dry thornveld and broadleaved woodland, singing a wonderful up-and-down, whistled "*whee-cheee-chooo-cheeera*" but also gives other whistles and grating sounds.

BLACK-BACKED PUFFBACK

FEMALE

MALE

Brown-crowned Tchagra L: 17 cm (6·5")

This species is smaller than Black-crowned Tchagra, has a black line above the white eyebrow, a brown central crown and buff underparts. It is a common and widespread resident in Kruger but prefers the dense thickets that predominate in the western half of the park. Brown-crowned Tchagra is more terrestrial than Black-crowned Tchagra, bouncing on the ground between thickets. It has a descending aerial display during which its wings flutter and make a *"prrrrrp"* rattling sound, before it sings a rapid series of 15–20 descending *"chee-ree"* notes as it returns to the ground.

BROWN-CROWNED TCHAGRA

BLACK-CROWNED TCHAGRA

☐ **Brubru** L: 13 cm (5")

This small, tree-loving, mostly black-and-white bush-shrike has a strong chestnut stripe running from the shoulders to the flanks; males are more brightly coloured than females. Its larger size, white eyebrow and horizontal posture distinguish it from the similar Chinspot Batis (*page 128*). The Brubru is a common resident throughout Kruger, favouring woodland, and joining mixed species flocks to hunt for insects. The call is remarkably like a telephone – a ringing, burry *"preeeeee"* – with some associated clicks and whistles.

☐ **Orange-breasted Bush-Shrike**
L: 19 cm (7·5")

This colourful bush-shrike is yellow and green with a bright orange chest. It is similar to the larger Grey-headed Bush-Shrike, but has a less robust bill and dark eyes. It also has prominent yellow eyebrows and a blackish patch in front of each eye. Juveniles also have a dark eye but lack the yellow eyebrows of the adult and have an all-greyish head. The Orange-breasted Bush-Shrike is a common and widespread resident in woodland throughout Kruger, creeping slowly through the mid-canopy of trees, hunting insects and small vertebrates. It is often first detected by its loud, ringing *"what-to-tooo-dooo"* song and scolding *"skeeeeet"* calls and clicks.

☐ **Grey-headed Bush-Shrike** L: 26 cm (10")

A striking, large and robust bush-shrike with a massive head and a chunky, hook-tipped bill. This species has a bright yellow eye and entirely grey head with pale lores (in front of the eye), differentiating it from the similar but daintier Orange-breasted Bush-Shrike. The shy Eastern Nicator (not illustrated) is similar in shape but can be distinguished by its green rather than grey head. The Grey-headed Bush-Shrike is a common and widespread resident in Kruger's woodlands and riverine forests, but is less abundant than Orange-breasted Bush-Shrike. It keeps to the canopy, hunting large insects and small vertebrates, including lizards, chameleons, snakes and baby birds, and sometimes creates a 'larder' by impaling prey on thorns. A low, prolonged sorrowful *"whhooooooo"* song given up to 50 times in succession earns it the appropriate local name of 'ghostbird'.

Gregarious, striking and attractive birds, some of which appear rather cartoon-like, that are often seen hunting from perches.

☐ White-crested Helmet-Shrike L: 18 cm (7")

A gregarious, black-and-white helmet-shrike with a bouffant-like white-and-grey crest and piercing yellow eyes and eye-wattles. It flies floppily from tree to tree, revealing a conspicuous pied pattern. Although a common and widespread resident in Kruger, it seems to be more numerous in winter (June–August). It is found mainly in a variety of woodland types, favouring areas along dry riverbeds, with close-knit parties of 5–10 birds foraging restlessly in trees and close to the ground in mixed or single-species flocks.

☐ Retz's Helmet-Shrike L: 20 cm (8")

This sociable, mostly black-and-brown helmet-shrike has piercing orange eyes, red legs and eye-wattles, and an orange-tipped red bill. It is resident and uncommon in Kruger but it can be nomadic. Small, tight flocks of 3–7 birds work co-operatively during the breeding season to raise chicks; outside the breeding season loose flocks of up to 30 birds can be seen foraging together. It may form flocks with White-crested Helmet-Shrikes, but tends to be less common and less conspicuous, preferring more densely wooded environments. The calls are harsh and grating. The Thick-billed Cuckoo (not illustrated), which is very rare in Kruger, uses the Retz's Helmet-Shrike as its host species.

ADULT

IMMATURE

WHITE-CRESTED HELMET-SHRIKE

◻ **Southern White-crowned Shrike** L: 24 cm (9")

An unmistakable gregarious, bulky, large-headed, vanilla-and-brown shrike with a big white cap above a dark brown mask and shawl. This species is widespread and uncommon throughout Kruger's drier woodlands and savannah, with a population of some 8,000, and can be nomadic. It may form the core of open-country mixed-species flocks, and has been recorded following hornbills and eating prey they disturb. However, it generally searches for invertebrates from a sentinel perch, dropping down to pick prey off the ground before returning to the same position. It is a co-operative breeder, with 2–6 helpers assisting the alpha pair. The calls are a repeated, shrill, plover-like *"kleeew-keeuw"*, as well as softer mewing notes.

☐ Violet-backed Starling L: 17 cm (6·5")

A small starling with dramatically different-looking sexes, although both have a distinctive lemon-yellow eye and a dark bill. The male is stunningly iridescent, varying from brilliant violet to reddish-purple depending on the light, except for the pure white belly and vent; it may look almost black-and-white in harsh light. The female has a brown-streaked white belly and darker, brown-streaked upperparts. A female could be confused for a thrush or a chat, but is usually accompanied by the unmistakable male, and has a long-winged, sharp-billed, square-tailed shape and flies farther and higher. This intra-African migrant is a common spring and summer (October–April) breeder in Kruger, where it inhabits lush savannah and riverine forests. It feeds opportunistically on berries and insects, particularly favouring winged termites. It nests in tree holes and other cavities where it may become a victim of brood parasites such as Lesser Honeyguide (*page 110*).

FEMALE

MALE

☐ Red-winged Starling

L: 31 cm (12")

A large, long-tailed, dark starling with striking chestnut windows in the wings, especially in flight. The male has glossy blackish plumage, whereas the female has a streaked dark grey head and breast. This species is a widespread and common resident around rocky cliffs and escarpments, and has also adapted to breeding on buildings in some camps, such as Olifants. It feeds on insects, fruits and nectar. The calls are a loud, liquid, oriole-like *"wher-teooo"*, although it also sings other musical notes.

MALE

RED-WINGED STARLING

FEMALE

Glossy-starlings are hole-nesters, and will aggressively usurp cavities from barbets, woodpeckers and woodhoopoes, or breed opportunistically in the nests of larger birds such as ibises.

BURCHELL'S STARLING

☐ Meves's Starling L: 34 cm (13")

This large, long-legged starling is similar to Burchell's Starling, being bright glossy blue-purple overall with a black face, but has a smaller body and a very long and graduated tail. It is common in lush savannah from the Levuvu River north, where Burchell's Starling is rare. It eats insects, fruits and flowers, and hunts on the ground in small groups where its long, floppy tail gives it a distinctive appearance.

CAPE GLOSSY STARLING

☐ Burchell's Starling L: 32 cm (13")

A large, long-tailed, blue-purple glossy-starling with subtly barred wings, black face, and a round-tipped, not graduated, tail. Meves's Starling is smaller-bodied, with a proportionately longer, graduated tail. Burchell's Starling is a common resident south of Shingwedzi in drier thornveld, and at camps, where it is tame and approachable. It feeds on the ground and low in trees, searching mainly for invertebrates, small vertebrates and fruits.

☐ Greater Blue-eared Starling
L: 22 cm (8·5")

Similar to Cape Glossy Starling, but can be differentiated by its blackish ear patch and contrasting royal blue flanks and belly. The upperside is glossy green, with two rows of neat black spots across the wing. This starling is a widespread and common resident in woodland and camps throughout Kruger, where it may be seen foraging for invertebrates, flowers and fruits, although it is more often seen scavenging at picnic sites. The call is a distinctive cat-like, nasal *"squuee-aar"*.

☐ Cape Glossy Starling L: 23 cm (9")

A medium-sized, yellow-eyed, blue-green starling that lacks a dark face (but does have a blackish stripe through the eye), and has rather uniform (not dark blue) flanks and belly and a bluer head and neck. Overall, this species is more uniformly coloured than the similar Greater Blue-eared Starling. It is a widespread and common resident throughout Kruger, favouring savannah in arid thornveld, and is a frequent scavenger at camps and rest stops. When not begging for handouts, it feeds on a range of invertebrates and fruits, and has been known to follow ungulates and prey on insects they disturb, as well as to glean skin parasites, such as ticks, off large mammals. The call is a cheerful *"chee-chee-cher"*.

Oxpeckers are strange relatives of starlings that feed exclusively from the bodies of large mammals, consuming mainly blood, ticks and other ectoparasites, and earwax. There is some debate as to whether the interactions between oxpeckers and mammals is mutually beneficial, with the birds obtaining a blood-filled meal while ridding large mammals of harmful parasites, but the fact that the birds also feed on open wounds, and may deliberately keep wounds open, suggests that they are actually true parasites. Both species of oxpecker may breed co-operatively, with helpers assisting related birds to raise young. Like starlings, oxpeckers are hole-nesters.

JUVENILE

☐ Yellow-billed Oxpecker L: 22 cm (9")

The canary-yellow bill with a red-tip, red eye and pale rump on an otherwise brown bird is diagnostic. Although juveniles lack the bright coloration of adult birds, they can be distinguished from juvenile Red-billed Oxpeckers by their pale rump. The Yellow-billed Oxpecker became extinct in South Africa by 1910 due to a combination of rinderpest wiping out buffaloes and poisoning by arsenic-based cattle dips. Remarkably, it recolonized naturally in 1979, once the dips were banned and African Buffalo numbers had recovered. This oxpecker is now widespread in the northern half of Kruger and although still uncommon, numbers are slowly increasing and its range is spreading southwards. It roams in small groups feeding off large ungulates, particularly buffaloes, giraffes and both rhino species. This species is reliant on conservation areas, but will also forage on domestic animals when it strays outside parks. The flight call is a short, harsh buzz.

☐ Red-billed Oxpecker L: 20 cm (8")

A slim, short-billed, short-legged plain brown bird with a diagnostic all-red bill and red eyes surrounded by fleshy yellow wattles. Juveniles lack bright coloration but, like adults, have a uniform brown rump and back (not pale as in Yellow-billed Oxpecker). This species is a common and widespread resident in Kruger, although numbers have declined outside protected areas. Small flocks move between large mammals with an undulating, swooping flight, settling on an animal in much the same way as a woodpecker lands on a tree. In flight, it gives a swizzling-crackle call.

JUVENILE

143

Sunbirds are small, active birds with long, downcurved bills. Their nests are pendulous structures built exclusively by the females, which also undertake all the incubation. The small green cuckoos, Klaas's and sometimes Diederik Cuckoo (*pages 90–91*), occasionally parasitize sunbirds, laying eggs in their nests. Sunbirds are the ecological equivalent of hummingbirds, surviving mostly on nectar and invertebrates, with the latter being particular popular when protein is required for fast-growing chicks.

FEMALE

☐ **Marico Sunbird** L: 12 cm (4·5")

The male Marico Sunbird is the only green-hooded, dark-bellied sunbird in Kruger and has two iridescent bands across the upper breast – one deep purple and the other maroon. The female is grey-brown, streaked on the underparts, but lacks the dark throat of the similar female Scarlet-chested Sunbird. Marico Sunbird is a common resident throughout Kruger, feeding on nectar from flowers and hunting insects, using its long, downcurved bill.

MALE

☐ Scarlet-chested Sunbird

L: 14 cm (5·5")

A large, fast-moving, dark sunbird with a slim, curved bill. The very distinctive male is glossy velvet-black with a striking scarlet chest and a glossy green moustache. The female is grey-brown, heavily streaked underneath, with streaking becoming so dense that it becomes a black patch on the throat. This species is a common resident throughout Kruger, although there can be influxes when nectar is locally abundant. The calls are a loud series of piping *"tip"* and *"teeeuw"* notes.

FEMALE

NON-BREEDING MALE

MALE

☐ **Collared Sunbird** L: 10 cm (4")

A tiny, short-billed, green-backed, yellow-bellied sunbird. The male has a green throat and narrow purplish breast-band, whereas the female is duller with a yellow throat and lacks a breast-band. This species is a common resident throughout Kruger in lush savannah and riverine forest fringes. Although it eats more insects than other sunbirds, it is also an adept nectar-parasite, using its short bill to pierce the base of flowers and steal nectar without fulfilling the role of pollinator.

FEMALE

Although there is a high diversity of sunbird species in Africa, occurring in a wide range of habitats, current understanding is that the family evolved in Asia and then spread to Africa.

Although sunbirds are superficially similar to the unrelated hummingbirds (which occur only in the Americas), they cannot hover perfectly. However, if there is nowhere for them to perch, some species can remain stationary in the air for long enough to feed off nectar or catch insects or spiders.

MALE

☐ White-bellied Sunbird

L: 11 cm (4·5")

A small sunbird with a long, curved bill. The male has iridescent blue-green upperparts and head, a bold white belly and a broad, purplish breast-band. The female is uniformly grey-brown above and pale-grey below. This sunbird is a common and widespread resident throughout Kruger, but can also be nomadic in response to seasonal nectar sources. It is, however, easily dominated by larger sunbirds.

FEMALE

Sunbirds have thin, downcurved bills and long, tubular, brush-tipped tongues – adaptations for feeding on nectar. The frayed edges to the tongue enable the bird to 'suck' nectar from flowers using capillary action, and by repeatedly inserting and extracting the tongue this acts as a pump.

The songs of White-bellied Sunbirds sometimes include mimicry of Dark-capped Bulbul, Rattling Cisticola or other birds, although the reason for this is unknown.

MALE

Weavers are a large and diverse family of birds, and aptly named as many species build conspicuous and often elaborate and intricate woven nests.

☐ **Red-billed Buffalo-Weaver** L: 24 cm (9")

Buffalo-weavers are large, thickset weavers. The male Red-billed Buffalo-Weaver has dark plumage, red legs and a large, vermilion bill, whereas the female and juvenile are paler and streaky on the underparts. Both sexes show obvious white wing patches in flight. This species' status in Kruger is variable: although there are some birds present throughout the year, most disperse in winter (May–August) and return to breed in spring and summer (September–April). However, in drier years it may become nomadic. It is a fairly common, sociable bird, preferring drier woodlands that hold large trees for their sprawling and untidy communal nests. The breeding system is complex, and both polygyny (single male with several females) and co-operative breeding can occur. Although a number of birds share the nest, each individual defends a particular part against other buffalo-weavers, making for some fascinating interactions. Large raptors occasionally nest on top of buffalo-weaver nests, offering some protection. Buffalo-weavers forage on the ground, often in association with starlings, searching for insects, seeds and fruits.

Spectacled Weaver L: 16 cm (6·5")

A smallish, neat, slim-billed weaver with plain green wings and back, yellow underparts and a thin, black 'bandit's' mask surrounding the yellow eye. Both sexes have a light orange facial wash, and males have a black throat patch. Fairly common in riverside habitats throughout Kruger and is often first noticed by its distinctive downward *"tee-tee-tee-tee-tee"* calls. Although pairs are often seen, it is not a particularly gregarious species and neither forms flocks nor nests in large colonies. It is mostly insectivorous but will also eat nectar and fruits.

MALE

FEMALE

Thick-billed Weaver L: 18 cm (7")

This is a large, chunky, dark brown and 'shiny' weaver with a very large bill. The male has a black bill and a white dash on the forehead and mid-wing; the smaller female is heavily streaked on the underparts and has a horn-coloured bill. This is a scarce but widespread resident in Kruger, breeding in reedbeds and wetlands in spring and summer. In winter (June–August) some individuals form non-breeding flocks and move into woodland and forest or disperse outside the park. It forages for seeds, fruits and insects, often on the ground.

MALE

FEMALE

149

The three 'masked-weavers' are all polygynous (a male breeding with several females) and colonial breeders. The males jointly defend an area in which they build pendulous nests woven of grass, reed and palm strips. A female will inspect the nests of several males until she finds a favourite; she will then mate with the builder and lay eggs within his section of the colony. Colonial nesting is a defence mechanism against predators, although brood parasitism (when another bird species lays its eggs in the host's nest) by cuckoos still occurs. Masked-weavers all call a similar series of 'radio static' churring, buzzing and swizzling notes at their colonies.

FEMALE

MALE

☐ Lesser Masked-Weaver
L: 13 cm (5")

This masked-weaver is Kruger's only species with a whitish eye: look for the eye colour first on any weaver you see. It is also the most dainty and diminutive weaver in the park. In breeding plumage, the male's black mask extends well onto the crown. The female is nondescript, but has a distinctive pale eye and white belly. This species is a widespread and locally common resident in Kruger, and is found in many camps, favouring riverine thickets in arid savannah. Outside the breeding season it forms large, nomadic flocks that roam widely. It feeds on invertebrates, nectar, flowers, fruits and small seeds.

FEMALE

COLONIAL NESTS OF
VILLAGE WEAVER

☐ Southern Masked-Weaver
L: 14 cm (5.5")

A medium-sized, red-eyed masked-weaver with a slighter build than the robust Village Weaver. The male has a plain green back, and the female can be distinguished from female Village Weaver by its shorter, more delicate bill, brighter red eye and whiter belly. This species is a common resident throughout Kruger in drier woodland and also camps, where it feeds mainly on seeds but also eats fruits, buds, nectar and invertebrates.

☐ Village Weaver L: 16 cm (6.5")

This is Kruger's largest masked-weaver. The male is told by the heavily blotched black-and-yellow upperparts and black face; the female by the long bill, deep red-brown eyes and pale yellow eyebrows. It is an abundant resident of wetland, riverine and woodland areas throughout Kruger. Although naturally it feeds on seeds and invertebrates, it will gladly partake of an easy meal at a rest camp or picnic area. Camps also provide excellent nesting areas, as they have fewer predators.

MALE

MALE

151

FEMALE

MALE

NEST

■ Red-headed Weaver L: 15 cm (6")

The only weaver with an orange bill, dark brown back with yellowish margins to the wing, and a white belly. The breeding male is distinctive, having a bright red head and upper-breast, and a black mask, while the female and non-breeding male have a yellow head and breast. This is a widespread and fairly common resident in Kruger's woodlands, joining mixed-species flocks in winter (June–August). It spends more time foraging in trees than other weavers, but has a similar diet of invertebrates, seeds and fruits. It is a solitary nester, building a long-necked nest that is unusually untidy for a weaver, and is often found breeding in camps.

FEMALE

MALE NON-BREEDING

MALE BREEDING

☐ **Red-billed Quelea** L: 12 cm (4·5")

A small brownish, sparrow-like member of the weaver family with a mottled back and yellow or reddish bill, eye-ring and legs. When breeding, males develop a variable black mask and reddish wash to the rest of the head and upper breast, although in some individuals the mask is white. This species is highly nomadic in arid savannah and in wetter years can form huge flocks, earning it the name of 'feathered locust'. In such years, the population in Kruger may exceed 30 million, comprising some 60% of all the birds in the park! However, in drier years and in the winter (June–August) it occurs in much lower numbers. Queleas roost in single-species flocks, or with other seed-eaters in reedbeds and trees alongside rivers. When conditions are suitable, they breed in huge colonies that attract a variety of predators. Adults feed primarily on seed, and can strip vast areas of seeding grass in hours; outside parks they are considered an agricultural pest.

MALE NON-BREEDING/ FEMALE

MALE NON-BREEDING

Southern Red Bishop L: 13 cm (5")

A small, rotund, sparrow-like bird. The breeding male shows an unmistakable mix of velvety vermilion and black, whereas the female and non-breeding male are nondescript, mainly identified by their small size, short tail, and strong buff eyebrow. This is a widespread resident in Kruger and, although uncommon, numbers are increasing. It is always found close to water in the summer (December–March), breeding colonially in reedbeds and swampy grassland, but disperses into the bush in the winter (June–August).

White-winged Widow L: 15 cm (6")

A finch-like bird with a longish tail. The breeding male is mostly jet-black but has yellow shoulder patches and a white flash in the wing, obvious in flight, and a pale bill. Non-breeding males and females are plain and rather nondescript. It is a widespread resident in Kruger, breeding in rank grasslands and marshy edges in summer (December–March), at other times forming mixed flocks with other birds in savannah, feeding mostly on seeds.

MALE NON-BREEDING/FEMALE

■ Red-collared Widow

L: 12 cm (4·5") (breeding male 25 cm (10"))

The breeding male is jet-black and develops a 13 cm (5") long floppy, graduated tail and a crimson collar, whereas females and non-breeding males are smaller with unstreaked underparts and a yellowish eyebrow. This widow is a widespread resident in Kruger, especially in the south of the park. It breeds in tall, wet grassland and is uncommonly encountered in wet years, but less frequently in drier years. Outside the breeding season it forms mixed flocks with others bishops in savannah, feeding mainly on seeds.

Male bishops and widows will mate with as many females as possible, and, other than providing a nest, play no role in parental care. In the breeding season, males moult from drab brown into colourful plumage, making them more likely targets for predators. The males that survive the attentions of predators are clearly the fittest and those that get to pass on their genes.

Waxbills are small finches that are inconspicuous despite their bright coloration.

☐ Blue Waxbill L: 13 cm (5")

This waxbill is readily identified by its entirely sky-blue underparts, rump and tail, silver-pink bill and grey-brown upperparts. The female is paler than the male, and juveniles are mostly grey-brown with a powder-blue wash to the face. It is a common and widespread resident in a variety of habitats in Kruger, favouring drier woodlands close to permanent water where it regularly comes to drink, often dispersing during perods of drought. It feeds mainly on grass seeds but will also take insects, and frequently gives a loud and distinctive high-pitched *"tsee-tsee"* call, especially when flushed.

☐ Red-billed Firefinch L: 10 cm (4")

Firefinches are small, thickset, thick-billed ground birds. Three species occur in Kruger, of which the Red-billed Firefinch is by far the most common, and readily identified by its pinkish bill. African Firefinch (not illustrated) has a slaty crown and a steel-blue bill, and Jameson's Firefinch (not illustrated) has a pinkish head and steel-blue bill. The Red-billed Firefinch is a widespread and common resident in the park, often feeding on grasses or on the ground close to thickets in woodland, or near water where it frequently drinks and bathes in the company of other small seed-eating birds. It has a melodic *"swee-tee-eeer"* song and gives a spitting, tinny *"prrrrrt"* call. This firefinch is the host of the nest parasite Village Indigobird (*page 162*).

☐ Common Waxbill L: 12 cm (4·5")

A finely barred, grey-brown waxbill with a waxy red bill, a scarlet 'bandit's' eye-mask, diffuse reddish belly patch, and dark under the tail. The sexes are alike but juveniles are dull-brown, with a dark bill. This is a common and widespread resident in Kruger, favouring long grass near wetlands, but also ventures into camps and woodland, where it feeds primarily on seeds. To protect its eggs and young from predators, the Common Waxbill builds a remarkable nest with a false entrance and disguises it with animal scats and fur. However, this deception does not fool the brood-parasitic Pin-tailed Whydah (*page 160*), which uses this waxbill as its main host species.

COMMON WAXBILL

BLUE WAXBILL

JUVENILE

JUVENILE

RED-BILLED FIREFINCH

FEMALE

☐ **Cut-throat Finch** L: 12 cm (4·5")

A small, heavily scaled and barred brownish waxbill, males having a characteristic scarlet throat-band, which gives the species its name. It is an inconspicuous and uncommon resident in Kruger, most numerous in the northern half of the park. It pairs up for breeding and constructs its nest within the old used nests of other birds such as weavers, buffalo-weavers and woodpeckers. Outside the breeding season it often joins flocks of other seed-eaters.

☐ **Bronze Mannikin** L: 9 cm (3·5")

This is a tiny, rotund, fast-moving waxbill with a stubby, greyish bill, brown upperparts with a darker bronzy head and breast, and an iridescent green shoulder patch. The strongly contrasting underparts are white with dark bars on the flank and under the tail. Juveniles are buffy-brown with a dark bill. This species is common and widespread in Kruger, particularly in the south. It is a gregarious seed-eater, most often seen feeding in the grassy verges of wetlands, woodlands and riverine areas, and moves locally depending on the availability of seed.

☐ **Green-winged Pytilia** L: 13 cm (5")

A distinctive waxbill with a red bill, rump and tail, olive-green back and wings, grey nape, and barred underparts. The male has an orange-red forehead and throat, and a golden-green band across the upper breast. The more subdued female lacks the breast-band and has an all-grey head, and juveniles are similar but have a dark bill. This is a common and widespread resident throughout Kruger but favours drier woodland with permanent water to which it comes to drink. It feeds on seeds and insects. The Green-winged Pytilia is the host of the brood-parasitic Long-tailed Paradise-Whydah (*page 161*).

GREEN-WINGED PYTILIA

MALE FEMALE

CUT-THROAT FINCH

FEMALE

MALE

BRONZE MANNIKIN

IMMATURE

ADULT

JUVENILE

159

Whydahs and indigobirds (*page 162*) are finch-like brood parasites of waxbills. In non-breeding plumage they are cryptic and difficult to identify, but in the breeding season male whydahs develop long tails and bold plumages, while male indigobirds become black. A remarkable feature of these birds is that the mouth spots of their chicks (revealed when they beg for food) mimic those of the chicks of their host, helping to fool the host into believing that they are raising one of their own offspring.

MALE BREEDING

MALE NON-BREEDING/FEMALE

Pin-tailed Whydah

L: 13 cm (5") (breeding male 34 cm (13·5"))

The breeding male is a striking pied bird with a bright red bill: it has a small body but sports a 21 cm (8") long fine, wispy tail. The buff-brown female and non-breeding male have a reddish bill and a distinctive face pattern, and do not have a long tail. Female and non-breeding male Shaft-tailed Whydahs (not illustrated) look similar but have a more buffy and diffuse face-pattern – however this species is scarce in Kruger. Female and non-breeding male Long-tailed Paradise Whydahs have a more contrasting head pattern, white rather than buff on the face, and a black bill. The Pin-tailed Whydah is a common and widespread resident in Kruger, inhabiting woodland, grassland and camps. It is much more obvious in spring and summer (October–March) when males moult into their breeding plumage and display by fluttering above a female, bobbing up and down and repeatedly singing a high-pitched song, and also giving simpler "*chip-chip-chip*" notes. This seed-eater is highly territorial and aggressive, and has been known to kill other birds that it considers to be competitors.

☐ **Long-tailed Paradise-Whydah** L: 15 cm (6") (breeding male 36 cm (14"))

The breeding male is unmistakable, having buff, chestnut and black plumage and a 21 cm (8") long tail with both short and bulging, and long, tapering, dagger-like feathers, which, from the side, looks thick and arched. Females and non-breeding males have a strongly contrasting black-and-white head, including a dark 'C' mark under the ears, a blackish bill, a pale tawny body, and black-and-white mottling on the wings and back. This species is a fairly common and widespread resident in drier woodland throughout Kruger, but remains cryptic and difficult to detect outside the breeding season. It makes dry *"chip"* calls and also mimics the calls and song of the Green-winged Pytilia (*page 158*), which it parasitizes. The whydah chicks are larger and more aggressive than pytilia chicks, guaranteeing the attention of their host 'parents'.

MALE BREEDING

MALE NON-BREEDING/FEMALE

☐ **Cinnamon-breasted Bunting** L: 15 cm (6")

A slender bunting with cinnamon underparts, black-and-brown mottled upperparts and a black-and-orange bill. The male's head is boldly striped black-and-white, while that of the female is less contrasting, with brown and buff stripes. This is a common and widespread resident in Kruger, occurring on rocky outcrops and in open woodland and grassland with a rocky component. It is often detected by its shrill, grating song.

☐ **Golden-breasted Bunting** L: 16 cm (6·5")

The combination of brilliant golden-yellow breast and yellow throat, boldly striped head, chestnut back and white wingbars easily identify this finch-like bird. When flushed, it shows bold white outer tail feathers as it flies away, and will often settle in a tree. The female looks similar to the male but is paler, and juveniles are duller still. This is a widespread and common resident throughout all of Kruger's woodlands, where it feeds on seeds, nectar and insects. It has a buzzy, nasal call and a cheerful *"toodletee chip-chip-chip"* song.

☐ **Village Indigobird** L: 12 cm (4·5")

In Kruger, this finch-like bird always has a red bill and red legs (farther north in its range the bill and legs can be much paler). The breeding male is entirely shiny black, but females and non-breeding males are brown and streaky-headed, resembling female and non-breeding male whydahs. However, the Pin-tailed Whydah (*page 160*) always has dark legs, and other, rarer, indigobirds (none illustrated) always have pale pinkish-white bills. The Village Indigobird is a widespread and uncommon resident, although it is the most frequently encountered indigobird species in Kruger. It parasitizes the Red-billed Firefinch (*page 156*), mimicking its song and calls.

MALE NON-BREEDING/FEMALE

MALE BREEDING

Yellow-fronted Canary L: 12 cm (4·5")

A smallish canary, bright yellow below with a strong head pattern, including a bright yellow stripe above the eye, a yellow cheek and a black moustache. The larger, greener-faced, and heavier-billed Brimstone Canary (not illustrated) occurs in the southwest of Kruger but is rare; and the much paler Lemon-breasted Canary (not illustrated) is rare and very local from Pafuri north. The Yellow-fronted Canary is a common and widespread resident in woodland and grassland throughout Kruger, where it feeds on grass and shrub seeds, nectar and invertebrates.

FEMALE

CINNAMON-BREASTED BUNTING

MALE

GOLDEN-BREASTED BUNTING

MALE

☐ Crested Guineafowl L: 46–52 cm (18–20")

A large but small-headed, black, ground bird, perfectly lined with rows of hundreds of bluish-white spots. It has a plumed 'toupee' above the naked face, and a distinctive ivory-coloured bill and blood-red eye. In flight, its darker plumage and pale patch in the wing distinguish it from the Helmeted Guineafowl (*page 65*). This species is locally common only along the Levuvu River in Kruger's far north (especially Pafuri), and rare elsewhere, such as in the far eastern Lebombo range. It prefers thick and wet riverine forest where it forages on the ground for berries, seeds and plant matter – and has a fascinating habit of associating with Vervet Monkeys, following troops and foraging on dropped fruits and faeces. The call is similar to that of the Helmeted Guineafowl, but with a more tinny quality.

Due to their constant busyness, guineafowl are considered as symbols of industry and are revered by traditional societies. They are also thought to be protectors, and despite their tastiness, are seldom killed for the pot.

☐ Purple-crested Turaco L: 43 cm (17")

This unmistakable large, horizontal, slender, long-necked bird of the treetops, has a dark blue tail and wings, an iridescent deep-purple crest, a pale rusty-orange upper back, an olive-pink suffusion to the underparts, an iridescent green face and a scarlet eye-ring. In flight, the wings are fiery red, making this one of Kruger's most striking birds. It is common in the park, with an estimated population of at least 4,000, and favours dense woodland, particularly along usually dry riverbeds. It clambers acrobatically along branches searching for fruits and insects, often leaning forward with its head in a dipped position. The call is a distinctive and characteristic croaking *"khoh-khoh-khoh-khoh…."* that gets progressively louder before stopping suddenly.

Although the coloration in the plumage of birds comes from a variety of widespread pigments like carotenoids, turacos have two unique pigments: turacin, comprising 6% copper, giving them richer and more vibrant red coloration; and turacoverdin, which gives them their greener hues.

☐ **Brown-headed Parrot** L: 24 cm (9")

This smallish green parrot has yellow underwings and
a plain brown head (although immatures are duller).
The much larger (34 cm) and more robust Grey-headed
Parrot (not illustrated) is very localized in Kruger,
mostly from Punda Maria north, and is told by its green
underwings, massive all-pale bill, and red shoulder
patches and 'boots'. Meyer's Parrot (not illustrated) is
scarce along the Limpopo and has an all-brown back
and wings. The Brown-headed Parrot is fairly common
throughout Kruger, with an estimated population of
2,500, with birds moving locally to take advantage of
fruiting trees. Loud, screeching, high-pitched, metallic
calls often draw attention to their presence in fruiting
trees or in flight. Although this bird is not threatened,
Kruger is a crucial area for its conservation in South
Africa, with numbers declining outside the park due to
habitat loss and trapping for the cage-bird trade.

☐ African Green-Pigeon L: 30 cm (12")

A plump, mainly green pigeon with a grey mantle and dull burgundy shoulders. The bill is whitish with a red base, the eyes are pale, and vent, 'boots' and wing edgings are yellow. This is a fairly common species in thicker woodland and riverine forest in Kruger, and often first detected by a strange and rather amusing call that involves whinnying clicks, whistles, cackles and growls. It is locally nomadic, depending on food availability, with groups of up to 30 sometimes congregating in fruiting trees, especially figs. They clamber around clumsily like parrots but can be infuriatingly well camouflaged in the canopy of tall trees, their presence often only being revealed by slight movements. When disturbed, they explode from a tree and fly fast and direct.

MALE

☐ **Trumpeter Hornbill** L: 66 cm (26")

A strikingly large, mostly black hornbill with a white belly, rump, underwing coverts, and trailing edge to the wing. It is easily identified by the huge grey-brown casque above the bill, longer in the male, and pinkish naked skin around the eye. Pairs and small groups are locally common in riverine forest fringes of larger rivers in Kruger, and it is particularly numerous at Pafuri. Its presence is often first detected by far-carrying, baby-like wailing "*whaaaaaa waa waa*" calls. This hornbill is mostly a fruit-eater, favouring the fruits of jackalberries, figs and ironwoods, but also catches invertebrates and small vertebrates, particularly when feeding young chicks that need additional protein as they develop.

FEMALE

☐ Narina Trogon L: 32 cm (13")

Trogons are secretive, long-tailed, large-headed, upright birds of the lower forest canopy. This spectacular species is mostly iridescent green, with a scarlet belly and broad yellow bill. The male has a green face and throat (brown on the female). The Narina Trogon is an uncommon resident in its riverine forest and thicket habitat, with a population of approximately 500 individuals in Kruger. The far north (Pafuri–Limpopo) and the Sabie River are the best areas to search. It sits upright and stationary in the forest canopy, watching for prey and then flying fast and direct to a new perch, showing a white underside to the tail. Territorial males give a series of soft, deep and throaty *"huooo-huooo"* calls, with more emphasis on the second syllable, particularly during the breeding season in the spring and summer (September–Februrary). This trogon competes with woodpeckers, barbets, woodhoopoes, oxpeckers, glossy-starlings and hornbills for nest holes.

MALE

FEMALE

MALE

Greenbuls and brownbuls are large, relatively inconspicuous relatives of the more familiar bulbuls (see Dark-capped Bulbul, *page 118*).

☐ Sombre Greenbul L: 18 cm (7")

A fairly long-tailed, rather nondescript, uniform drab-olive bird, slightly paler on the belly, with striking pale eyes (although juveniles have dark eyes and a small yellow gape). It is a common resident throughout Kruger in the mid-storey and canopy of riverine forest and thickets, but is quite secretive and often first detected by its loud and shrill *"Willie! Come out and play with me"* song, ending with a nasal *"sca-a-ared"*. It feeds primarily on fruits, but will also eat insects.

☐ Yellow-bellied Greenbul L: 22 cm (9")

Although rather nondescript, this relatively large and bulky greenbul has greenish upperparts and yellowish underparts, including the underside of the tail. However, it has distinctive red eyes with a broken white eye-ring, a fairly large, pointed bill, a small, shaggy crest and shows yellowish underwings in flight. It is a locally common resident in a few localities in Kruger, particularly in the Punda Maria–Pafuri area and in the Nwambiya Sand Forest. It favours thickets and forest where it forages on fruits and insects, and is often first detected by its nagging, puppy-like *"yeehn-yeehn-yeehn"* call and various chattering notes.

☐ Terrestrial Brownbul L: 19 cm (7.5")

A dull brown, gregarious bird with dark red eyes and a whitish throat. It favours thickets and riverine forest where it scuffles through the undergrowth, flicking dead leaves in search of invertebrates and small vertebrates. It is a common and widespread resident throughout Kruger, usually occurring in small groups of 4–6 individuals, and gives a series of harsh, nasal *"ugk-ugk-ugk-ugk"* notes.

SOMBRE GREENBUL

YELLOW-BELLIED GREENBUL

☐ White-browed Robin-Chat L: 18 cm (7")

A large, eye-catching, thrush-like robin-chat with striking orange underparts and collar, and a dark mask and crown split by broad white eyebrows; the back and wings are olive-grey. This is a common resident in Kruger, favouring thick woodland and riverine forest, and becoming particularly confiding in camps. Its vocalizations are distinctive: basic variations of a bold, duetted *"puu-deet, puuu-deet, puuu-deet"* song getting louder and louder and rising to a crescendo, and can incorporate varied, jumbled notes and some mimicry when giving the alarm call. Territories are defended vigilantly, even against snakes, and intruding male robin-chats may be bludgeoned nearly to death.

The White-browed Robin-Chat is one of the hosts of the parasitic Red-chested Cuckoo (*page 87*), and if you are very lucky you might see an adult feeding a much larger, dark and heavily barred fledgling.

Red-capped Robin-Chat
L: 16 cm (6·5")

This is the most vibrantly coloured of the robin-chats, with tail, underparts, throat and face all vivid pumpkin-orange. The cap is dull, the back and wings steel-blue, and the central tail feathers are dark. It is locally common in riverine forest and thicket habitat, particularly in the Limpopo-Levuvu, Shingwedzi and Sabie river catchments, and is easily found in Letaba and Skukuza camps. It is often first detected by its distinctive plaintive, trembling *"creee-craww"* contact call, and other typically fluty robin-chat vocalizations, including much mimicry. However, its secretive nature means that it can be hard to find when silent, notably during the winter (June–August).

White-throated Robin-Chat
L: 15 cm (6")

A medium-sized robin-chat with a slaty-grey crown and back separated from black wings by a white bar across the shoulder, and with a white eyebrow contrasting with a face-mask. The throat and belly are white, fading into amber-orange on the vent and in the outer tail feathers. This species is an uncommon and secretive resident in Kruger, favouring woodland close to watercourses. Like all robin-chats it tends to stay low, feeding mostly on the ground and singing at eye-level or below. The high-pitched, melodious song and calls include extensive mimicry of other birds.

African Dusky Flycatcher
L: 12 cm (4·5")

A small, upright, dumpy bird, with typical flycatcher habits, but a shorter tail and wings and slightly darker plumage than Spotted Flycatcher (*page 130*). In comparison, it also lacks distinct streaking on the crown and forehead, but may have faint mottling on the breast, and short eyebrows. Kruger's small resident population is augmented in winter (June–August) by many individuals that move in from the nearby escarpment forests; overall it is uncommon. This flycatcher prefers thick woodland and riverine forest, where high-pitched *"tzeet"* and *"tsirit"* calls betray its presence.

Green-backed Camaroptera
L: 13 cm (5")

A small, rotund warbler that often leans forward on a perch and cocks its short tail. This species has red eyes, a green back and nape and grey-white underparts. It is a common resident in low thickets and riverine areas throughout Kruger, hopping about searching for small insects. Usually detected by its call, the two common vocalizations are a nasal *"meehrrp"* call that gives it the alternative name of 'bleating-warbler', and a strident, repeated, snapping *"strik-strik-strik-strik-strik"*.

☐ African Paradise-Flycatcher L: 17 cm (6·5") (breeding male 34 cm (13·5"))

A remarkable, often conspicuous, rusty-backed and rusty-tailed flycatcher with a crest. The breeding male has incredibly long, 17 cm (7"), central tail feathers that trail like the ribbon of a rhythmic gymnast. Both sexes have a dark crest and a blue eye-ring and bill, although juveniles are duller. This is a common spring and summer (September–March) breeding visitor throughout Kruger, with some individuals overwintering. It prefers lush savannah and riverine forest and is very vocal, often giving a repeated, grating *"gee-zwee"* call and a sweet melodic *"willie-willie-willie-wee-wooo"* song.

MALE

IMMATURE FEMALE

☐ **Southern Boubou** L: 23 cm (9")

A plump dark-backed and dark-eyed bush-shrike with a pale throat, buff underparts and a striking white stripe on the dark wing. The Black-backed Puffback (*page 132*) is superficially similar but is smaller and has a red eye. In the far north, the Southern Boubou is replaced by the similar Tropical Boubou (not illustrated), which is paler below. It is a common resident in most of Kruger but is shy and skulking, creeping stealthily through thickets, usually with a horizontal posture, hunting invertebrates and small vertebrates. Boubous are usually heard before they are seen, giving loud, distinctively hollow, ringing duets: *"wheeet-whee-do-do-do"*, single loud *"wheee"* notes, and a rattling scold like the vibrating of a seed-pod being shaken.

Southern Boubous can be inventive foragers and indulge in some unusual tactics to get a meal – including pulling bark from trees to search for geckos, wedging snails between branches to enable them to tear out the flesh, and even occasionally hawking flying insects.

IMMATURE

ADULT

WHITE-BACKED
VULTURE

LAPPET-FACED
VULTURE

HOODED VULTURE

IMMATURE

WHITE-HEADED
VULTURE

CAPE VULTURE

ADULT FEMALE

IMMATURE

STEPPE EAGLE

TAWNY EAGLE

IMMATURE

MARTIAL EAGLE

ADULT

BATELEUR

IMMATURE

178

BROWN SNAKE-EAGLE

WAHLBERG'S EAGLE

IMMATURE

AFRICAN HAWK-EAGLE

ADULT

BLACK-BREASTED
SNAKE-EAGLE

IMMATURE

AFRICAN
CROWNED EAGLE

VU ☐ Secretarybird

L: 120–140 cm (47–55") | WS: 190–220 cm (75–87")

The Sectretarybird is a very odd bird of prey in an ancient lineage and its own family. It is a tall, long-legged, crane-like, ground-loving raptor with distinctive quill-like plumes on its head and bright-red facial skin. In flight, the combination of dark trailing edge to the wing, diamond-shaped tail and long spatulate central tail projection is unmistakable. This bird is uncommon in Kruger, numbering about 300 individuals, and is declining throughout South Africa. It prefers open grasslands and savannahs, where it strides about searching for reptiles, small mammals and insects, which it bludgeons with its powerful legs.

The strange name of the Secretarybird was once thought to originate from the quills on its head bearing some resemblance to the quill pens used by an office secretary in times past. However, it is more likely that the name is a corruption of saqr-et-tair, the Arabic name for the bird, which translates as 'hunter-bird'. The Secretarybird is featured on the South African national coat of arms.

Raptors are declining dramatically throughout the continent, and Kruger is a crucial stronghold for many species. Unfortunately, even here they are at risk, with poachers often deliberately poisoning birds to delay authorities from discovering poached mammal carcasses. A single poisoning event can kill hundreds of individuals and can be catastrophic for these long-lived birds which take many years to reach maturity and produce only a small number of young each year. As a result, many of the species covered in this section of the book are unfortunately now threatened with extinction. Birds of prey are a crucial element of Kruger's ecosystem, with vultures disposing of carcasses, and other raptors hunting live prey. Because raptors in flight are best compared side-by-side, spreads featuring similar-looking soaring birds are shown on *pages 177–179*.

CR ☐ Hooded Vulture   L: 62–72 cm (24–28") | WS: 155–165 cm (61–65")

This is Kruger's smallest vulture, and is mostly brown with a small, naked pink head, sparsely covered with velvety white down. Adults have a diagnostic drooping slender black bill and blue eye-ring, which are visible at close quarters, but young birds have grey facial skin and brown rather than white down on the nape. In flight it has a rounded tail, and silvery flight feathers and flies on flat or slightly drooped wings. Within South Africa, this rare but conspicuous bird is virtually restricted to Kruger, where the population is estimated at 50–100 pairs. The Hooded Vulture is easily displaced from carcasses by larger and more aggressive vultures, although its fine bill allows access to meat that its competitors cannot reach.

IMMATURE   ADULT

EN ☐ **Cape Vulture** L: 96–115 cm (38–45") | WS: 225–260 cm (89–102")

This impressive vulture is creamy-white overall and much paler and generally larger than the otherwise similar White-backed Vulture, and glides with its wings slightly raised. At close range, the adults' honey-coloured eyes and a speckled stripe across the middle of each wing are distinctive features. The immature is heavily streaked (see *page 177*). The Cape Vulture is endemic to southern Africa and an uncommon visitor to Kruger, foraging in the park and returning to its breeding colonies on the escarpment, hundreds of kilometres away. The two patches of naked skin at the base of the neck are thought to be temperature sensors for detecting thermals.

CR ☐ **White-backed Vulture** L: 78–98 cm (31–39") | WS: 195–225 cm (77–89")

A fairly large, brownish vulture which, on the ground, can be seen to have a very long, sparsely downy neck. It is likely to be confused only with the much rarer Cape Vulture but is usually smaller and darker overall. In flight, adults show pale underwing coverts contrasting strongly with the darker body and a diagnostic white rump, most often visible when the bird is banking; immatures are more difficult to identify. Like Cape Vulture, it glides with its wings slightly raised. White-backed Vulture is by far the commonest vulture in Kruger, although the population in the park may only number 600–900 pairs. Loose breeding colonies are scattered in tall trees. This species is highly susceptible to poisoning.

IMMATURE

ADULT

EN ☐ **Lappet-faced Vulture**

One of the BIG 6

L: 115 cm (45") | WS: 250–290 cm (98–114")

This vulture, Africa's largest, has a massive, square, naked head with wrinkled loose flaps of skin ('lappets') on the face, and a bulky two-tone bluish-yellow bill. Adults are brown-backed with a brown-and-white-streaked chest and puffy white 'leggings'; immatures are all-brown. In flight, the massive size, very broad wings held flat or arched, white leggings, and, in adults, narrow white line towards the front of the wing characterize this leviathan of the skies. Like all the African vultures, this species is declining, and is an uncommon resident in Kruger, where the total population is estimated at about 250, with as few as 78 pairs breeding. Although it occurs throughout the park, it tends to favour areas with relatively sparse grass and tree cover, in the southern third of Kruger. However, birds range over vast areas and have incredible eyesight, frequently being seen at kills. On arrival at a carcass, this vulture tends to dominate the scene with its intimidating bulk. It hisses and scowls, opens its wings, and hops aggressively towards other scavengers. It will take on others far larger than itself, such as jackals and Marabou Storks, in order to maintain its status at a kill. While the bald head does not add to this bird's beauty, it is highly practical in avoiding feathers becoming soiled when the bird plunges its head into a carcass. Other vultures are often reliant on this species to open up parts of the carcass that their more dainty bills cannot breach. Individuals can eat up to 1·5 kg of meat at any one time.

CR ■ **White-headed Vulture** L: 84 cm (33") | WS: 200–230 cm (79–91")

A medium-sized, mostly dark brown vulture with an angular, naked, pink head and bulky, coral-coloured bill (although juveniles are all-brown). In flight the adults' white 'armpits' extend out as a stripe along the middle of the underwing. The larger females can be told from males by having all-white innermost flight feathers (secondaries). The 50–80 pairs that occur within Kruger represent the main South African population of this rare resident species. This vulture is often one of the first species to arrive at a carcass, where it dominates most other raptors except the much larger Lappet-faced Vulture. It has been known to steal the kills of eagles and sometimes hunts and kills small mammals, birds and reptiles.

ADULT

IMMATURE

EN ☐ Tawny Eagle
L: 65–75 cm (26–30") | WS: 160–190 cm (63–75")

This eagle can sometimes be identified solely by its combination of pale buffy coloration and large size. However, it is a variable species, and some individuals are dark brown, leading to confusion with summer migrant eagles that have brown plumage. It glides on flat or arched wings and is told from the larger Steppe Eagle by having a shorter gape that reaches to just below the centre of the pale eye, and from the rarer Lesser Spotted Eagle (not illustrated) by having puffy (rather than thin) 'leggings'. The Tawny Eagle is one of the commonest resident eagles in Kruger, with a population of more than 500 pairs. It scavenges, steals food from other predators, and preys on small vertebrates.

☐ Steppe Eagle L: 70–84 cm (28–33") | WS: 165–215 cm (65–85")
The Steppe Eagle is slightly larger than the Tawny Eagle, and never as pale as most adults. It also has a longer gape that extends to below the back of the dark eye, giving the bird a 'grinning' appearance. Immatures, which are more common than adults in Kruger, show a diagnostic white band along the middle of the underwing. This is an uncommon, non-breeding, late spring and summer (October–April) visitor to Kruger and feeds in much the same way as Tawny Eagle.

☐ Wahlberg's Eagle L: 53–61cm (21–24") | WS: 130–146 cm (51–57")
This is Kruger's smallest brown eagle, with a comparatively smaller head and weaker bill than the larger brown eagles, and a distinct short crest that gives the head a squared-off appearance. In flight it has a distinctive shape: almost like a crucifix, with straight-edged wings and a long, straight-edged tail that is generally held closed. Although pale (*below*) and intermediate morphs do occur, individuals with chocolate-brown plumage are most frequent. This species is a common intra-African migrant, with hundreds of pairs breeding in Kruger (between August and April). It hunts a broad range of vertebrate and insect prey, both from perches and on the wing, and has been known to kill competitors such as goshawks and owls.

TAWNY EAGLE

STEPPE EAGLE

One of the BIG 6

EN ☐ Martial Eagle

L: 78–84 cm (31–33") | WS: 188–260 cm (74–102")

This impressive eagle, with a short but prominent crest, is Africa's largest and one of the world's heaviest. The adult is uniform dark brown on the head, back and chest, and has a white belly with brown spots. The immature is pale on the head and chest, and the back is scaled greyish with white; confusion with immature African Crowned Eagle (*page 192*) is possible, but the underwing coverts of immature Martial Eagle are white, not creamy tan. It prefers wooded savannah habitats, and Kruger is a key refuge for this uncommon resident species, supporting a population of 150–250, including some 35–50 active nests. With a vast home range of some 144 km^2 they wander widely, often leaving Kruger, making them susceptible to persecution. These birds take 6–7 years to mature and have been recorded living until 17 years old. They lay only one egg in each clutch, and do not breed every year – and are therefore unable to recover quickly if their population crashes. Martial Eagles have extremely keen eyesight, and are able to detect prey from up to six kilometres away. They hunt mostly on the wing, attacking prey from above and feeding on anything from guineafowl to bustards, and from monitor lizards to small ungulates.

ADULT

IMMATURE

ADULT

☐ African Fish-Eagle

L: 63–73 cm (25–29") | WS: 200–240 cm (79–94")

One of the most distinctive large raptors in Africa, the African Fish-Eagle's mostly chestnut-and-white plumage and penetrating, fluty *"wheeee-ah-wheee"* call make it one of the icons of the African bush. Although immatures are scruffier than adults, they still have distinctive mottled dark brown and white blotching which is especially noticeable in flight. This species is a locally common resident in Kruger and is frequently seen around permanent watercourses and other wetlands. Pairs have a strong bond and are often seen together, but since suitable habitat is limited they are fiercely territorial and rivals sometimes interlock claws and plunge, open-winged, towards the ground in a cartwheeling motion. Such show-downs sometimes end in death. As its name suggests, this species feeds mainly on fish, which are caught with a graceful, shallow plunge to the water's surface. However, it will also eat birds and reptiles, and occasionally steals the catches of herons, storks and even Pied Kingfishers.

IMMATURE

ADULT

ADULT

☐ African Hawk-Eagle

L: 60–65 cm (24–26") | WS: 130–160 cm (51–63")

A medium-sized, boldly patterned, black-and-white eagle.
In flight, it holds its wings flat and adults show a unique pattern
of brown-and-white underwings with a thick black trailing edge,
and mostly white tail with a broad black terminal bar. However,
immature birds have entirely rufous underparts, including the
underwings (see *page 179*). This is a fairly common resident
in Kruger, where there is an estimated population of 350 pairs.
Although it will eat other vertebrates, it is primarily a bird hunter,
with francolins and guineafowls being favoured. Hawk-eagles
often hunt in pairs, with one acting as a decoy or 'flusher' while
the other strikes the victim; afterwards prey is shared.

EN ▢ Bateleur L: 55–70 cm (22–28") | WS: 180–185 cm (71–73")

This is a distinctive and colourful, very short-tailed eagle, although young birds are all-brown (see *page 178*). Adults are mostly black with a chestnut mantle and tail, grey shoulders, and a bright red face and legs. In flight, the female has a thin black trailing edge to the white wings, whereas the male has a broad black edge. The long, pointed wings are raised in a distinct 'V' when gliding, and the birds waver from side to side in a fashion that makes them look unstable. The Bateleur is a common resident in Kruger, with some 400–600 pairs – accounting for 85% of the South African population. Although it does hunt, about 70% of the diet of the birds in Kruger is carrion. Because it flies low, it is capable of finding small items of carrion, and is watched carefully by other scavengers as it is often the first to locate a carcass. No bird illustrates the need for large conservation areas better than the Bateleur: it was once common across South Africa, but poisoning and persecution have resulted in it now being almost restricted to large protected areas.

MALE

FEMALE

FEMALE
CHESTNUT-BACKED
MORPH

MALE
WHITE-BACKED
MORPH

The Zulus believed that the Bateleur was the first bird created by God, and that it symbolized life itself. It was therefore traditionally revered and afforded much protection.

VU ☐ African Crowned Eagle L: 90 cm (35") | WS: 130–160 cm (51–63")

A very large, crested, boldly marked eagle. The underparts are blotched and barred black and white, with a variable rufous wash across the breast. In flight, the underside shows strong barring, although immatures are paler and less distinctly marked than adults and have creamy-tan underwings. This species is an uncommon and localized resident in Kruger, favouring riverine forest. It has an undulating display flight coupled with a loud *"wheee-yooo, wheee-yooo, wheee-yooo"* call that often draws attention. Although smaller than the Martial Eagle (*page 188*), it is arguably more powerful. Its relatively short, broad wings give it excellent manoeuvrability in dense forest, where it hunts mostly primates, especially Vervet Monkeys. Birds have been reported to stalk prey for days, sometimes wounding it and then waiting for it to weaken before killing it.

☐ Black-breasted Snake-Eagle L: 63–68 cm (25–27") | WS: 160–178 cm (63–70")

A medium-sized eagle with brown-and-white plumage and yellow eyes. It is superficially similar to the Martial Eagle (*page 188*), but is smaller, and lacks spots on the white underparts (juveniles are mostly rufous). In flight, it has brown-barred white underwings, rather than all-brown as in Martial Eagle. This species is uncommon in Kruger, although its nomadic tendencies mean that numbers fluctuate. It sometimes hovers when hunting. It feeds mainly on snakes and has heavily scaled feet to help protect it if struck, but will also eat skinks, monitors and other small vertebrates.

☐ Brown Snake-Eagle

L: 71–76 cm (28–30") | WS: 150–165 cm (59–65")

A medium-sized dark-brown eagle with yellow eyes, a large, bulky, owl-like head, pale unfeathered legs and a brown-and-white-banded tail. Most immatures are paler than adults but at all ages the brown-and-silver underwing is distinctive in flight. This is a nomadic species which is fairly common in Kruger, although most individuals in the park are probably non-breeding visitors. It favours more wooded habitats than Black-breasted Snake-Eagle and mostly hunts from perches. As the name suggests it feeds mainly on snakes, including mambas, cobras and adders, landing on their head or spine and disabling them, but will also take other vertebrates.

Falcons have rounded heads, dark-eyes, relatively short legs and long wings that taper to a point. Other raptors such as hawks and eagles belong to a completely different and only distantly related family, and have paler eyes, shorter, rather rounded wings and longer legs.

Eurasian Hobby
L: 36 cm (14") | WS: 69–84 cm (27–33")

A small, dark-backed falcon with a dark hood and long, dark 'tear-drop' moustachial streaks and 'notch' behind the eye that contrast with the white cheeks and throat. The cere (fleshy area around the nostrils), eye-ring and legs are yellow. The underside is white with thick black streaks, and the 'trousers' and vent are pale rufous. Immatures have buff feather fringes. Confusion is possible with female Amur Falcon, but that species is smaller, has a pale buff vent, orange legs and cere, spotted underparts and white underwings. The Eurasian Hobby is an uncommon spring and summer (October–April) non-breeding visitor to Kruger, preying on large insects, such as dragonflies, as well as bats and fast-flying birds, often hunting at dawn and dusk. It feeds opportunistically and can gather in large groups.

VU Lanner Falcon
L: 46 cm (18") | WS: 90–110 cm (35–43")

This large, bulky, strong-flying falcon has relatively long, broad wings. It has the characteristic head pattern of most falcons – white face with a darker crown and strong black 'tear' marks – while the rusty cap that extends to the nape is diagnostic. Immatures are browner than adults, and are heavily blotched underneath, with a pale brown cap. Although the Lanner is uncommon in Kruger, it is the most frequently seen resident falcon. It usually breeds on cliff ledges, although birds can be seen anywhere in the park as they hunt on the wing, feeding mostly on birds which they either pursue in level flight or take on the ground.

LANNER FALCON

EURASIAN HOBBY

MALE

AMUR FALCON

☐ Amur Falcon L: 30 cm (12") | WS: 63–71 cm (25–28")

A small falcon with an orange-red cere, eye-ring and legs. The male is mainly sooty-grey with a chestnut vent, whereas the female is mostly greyish, with a speckled chest and buff to white vent. In flight the male appears bicoloured, with white underwing coverts and otherwise dark underparts, while the female is speckled grey on white, and has a barred tail. The immature is like the female but browner. This is a fairly common late spring and summer (November–April) non-breeding visitor to Kruger and is highly sociable and nomadic, flocks tracking local rainfall events. It feeds mainly on insects, hunting from a perch or by hovering, and frequently attends termite emergences (often after rain storms), where it can eat up to 20 termites per minute.

MALE

FEMALE

195

Rock Kestrel L: 32–39 cm (13–15") | WS: 68–79 cm (27–31")

This kestrel is mostly chestnut above with black spots, and with
a grey head, black-banded grey tail and black tips to the wings.
Immatures are browner and streakier than adults with a more
barred tail. The plumage of the scarce migrant Lesser Kestrel (not
illustrated) differs more obviously between the sexes: adult males
are unspotted above and have a blue-grey wing panel, whereas
females are heavily barred and look very similar to Rock Kestrel.
The Rock Kestrel is an uncommon breeding resident in Kruger,
most often encountered north of Shingwedzi. It hunts from a
perch or from the air, where it characteristically hovers, preying
on small birds, mammals, reptiles and insects.

Shikra L: 28 cm (11") | WS: 48–68 cm (19–27")

A small grey-and-white sparrowhawk with brown-barred
underparts. The unmarked upper tail and vibrant eye-colour
(deep red in the male, dark orange in the female) distinguish it
from other small hawks, but good views are required to be certain.
The immature is brownish and has a distinctive dark vertical throat-
stripe, but lacks the white rump of the immature Gabar Goshawk.
A common resident in Kruger, hunting lizards, insects and other
small prey from perches and occasionally on the wing.

Little Sparrowhawk L: 25 cm (10") | WS: 39–52 cm (15–20")

This is one of the world's smallest hawks and its tiny size should
prevent confusion with other similar species, although the white
spots on the tail are also diagnostic in both adults and juveniles.
An uncommon, secretive and inconspicuous resident of riverine
forest and thicker bush in Kruger. It is an extremely rapid flyer,
able to twist and turn through seemingly impenetrable thickets,
where it takes small birds, other vertebrates and insects.

African Goshawk L: 38–46 cm (15–18") | WS: 70 cm (28")

A medium-sized hawk with yellow eyes and legs, grey-brown
upperparts and brown-barred underparts: its size, grey cere (fleshy
area around the nostrils) and dark rump are distinctive. Immatures
(*right*) like other young hawks, but usually show white eyebrows
and spots (not bars) on the throat. Scarce in Kruger, where it seems
to prefer riverine forest, hunting for medium-sized birds such as
francolins and doves (occasionally rodents and insects). Its presence
is often revealed by its sharp *"chwik"* aerial display call, given every
2–3 seconds for over a minute at a time, sometimes well before dawn.

IMMATURE

SHIKRA

LITTLE SPARROWHAWK

SHIKRA

ROCK KESTREL

LITTLE SPARROWHAWK

ADULT

AFRICAN GOSHAWK

☐ Lizard Buzzard

L: 36 cm (14") | WS: 63–79 cm (25–31")

A small, stocky, greyish hawk with a distinctive pale throat marked by a vertical black stripe. It most similar to Gabar Goshawk, both having a broad white rump band in flight, but the throat streak, a pale band across the middle of the tail, and pale tail tips are diagnostic of the Lizard Buzzard. Despite its name, it is most closely related to sparrowhawks, but is shorter-legged and has a more powerful build. This species is an uncommon resident in Kruger, with an estimated population of 500 individuals. It is most frequently seen perched in the open, watching for prey, favouring grassland areas where it takes skinks, lizards, small snakes and other small vertebrates, and insects.

LIZARD BUZZARD

☐ Gabar Goshawk

L: 36 cm (14") | WS: 56–66 cm (22–26")

A small, slender, greyish hawk with a distinct grey head and chest and grey-barred underparts, and a dark bill and eyes (immatures are brownish – streaked on the breast and barred on the belly – and have pale eyes). It is most easily confused with smaller sparrowhawks, despite being most closely related to the chanting-goshawks, and also resembles the Lizard Buzzard, although it lacks that species' throat streak and distinctive tail band. A scarce, nearly all-black (melanistic) form comprises 6–14% of individuals in Kruger. This is a common resident in the park, with numbers increasing in March–July following an influx of immature birds, possibly related to post-breeding dispersal from elsewhere. A supreme bird hunter, both from perches and on the wing, it terrorizes waterholes and nesting colonies of weavers, queleas and bishops.

NORMAL FORM

MELANISTIC FORM

GABAR GOSHAWK

ADULT

DARK CHANTING-GOSHAWK

ADULT

GABAR GOSHAWK

IMMATURE

☐ Dark Chanting-Goshawk

L: 56 cm (22") | WS: 86–104 cm (34–41")

Chanting-goshawks are large, tall, long-tailed and long-legged, slaty-grey hawks. The legs and base of the bill are pink-orange. In flight, black tips to the dark upperwings and whitish underwings are distinctive. The immature is a brown, streaked version of the adult. This species is fairly common in well-wooded parts of Kruger, where there is a population of at least 200 pairs, particularly in the western parts of the park and especially around Pretoriuskop. Chanting-goshawks give a strong, gull-like *"kleeeu"* call and other piping whistles, hence their name. They feed on small vertebrates and large insects, and are known to follow Southern Ground-Hornbills (*page 107*) and Honey Badgers to prey on animals they flush.

GABAR GOSHAWK
IMMATURE

DARK CHANTING-GOSHAWK
IMMATURE

☐ Black-shouldered Kite

L: 30–35 cm (12–14") | WS: 82–94 cm (32–37")

A small powder-grey kite with a white tail, underparts and face, striking red eye, and black shoulders and flight feathers. Immatures are browner than adults, with a scalloped brown back and tawny chest. It is often seen perched up, or characteristically 'frozen' in hovering flight, looking down for prey. The much browner and longer-winged Rock Kestrel (*page 196*) is the only other small bird of prey to hover. The Black-shouldered Kite is an uncommon breeding species in Kruger, favouring open grassland where it hunts for insects and small vertebrates; numbers increase in years of rodent irruptions.

☐ Black Kite

L: 61 cm (24") | WS: 130–155 cm (51–61")

Kites are larger than falcons, but smaller than eagles. The Black Kite has long wings and a broad tail that spreads to a wide fan shape but looks forked when closed. It is all-brown (rather than black as its name would imply) with a distinctive yellow bill, and flies slowly, giving the impression that it is dangling in the air – and when banking characteristically twists its tail in the opposite direction to maintain balance. The African race of this very widespread Old World species is often called the Yellow-billed Kite, and is an abundant breeding migrant to Kruger between July and March, where it is found in most habitats. Much rarer in Kruger is the race that migrates from Eurasia, which differs in having a greyer head, more streaked body, squarer tail and black bill. The Black Kite will prey on almost anything, including carrion and road kills, and, if you are not careful, your lunch at one of the picnic stops, with surprisingly fast and powerful stoops. They habitually attend fires, foraging on hapless insects and other small prey that attempt to flee their impending doom.

BLACK KITE

BLACK-SHOULDERED KITE

IMMATURE

ADULT

AFRICAN HARRIER-HAWK

☐ African Harrier-Hawk

L: 66 cm (26") | WS: 140 cm (55")

A large, naked-faced grey hawk. The adult is superficially similar to a chanting-goshawk (*page 199*), but has a unique shape, with a long, angular head and broad wings, and a characteristically floppy flight between glides. The small bare yellow face (sometimes flushed red), white-banded black tail and underwing pattern are further diagnostic features. The immature is blotchy brown and eagle-like but has distinctive yellow-green facial skin and barred flight feathers. Although this species is a fairly common resident in Kruger, numbers do fluctuate from year to year. Harrier-hawks specialize in feeding on eggs and nestlings, although they will also take small vertebrates and insects. Their unique double-jointed ankle can bend backwards, allowing them access to nest holes and confined spaces, and they are often seen clambering around clumsily, wings half open, on cliffs and in trees when searching for prey, especially targetting weaver colonies.

Swifts are fast-flying, scimitar-winged birds with minute feet that do not allow them to perch like swallows and martins (see *pages 204–207*).

☐ African Black Swift L: 18 cm (7")

This is a dark, bulky, powerful, high-flying swift with a distinct white throat patch and contrasting greyish inner flight feathers (secondaries). The very similar Common Swift (not illustrated) has a smaller throat patch and lacks a pale panel in the wing. The African Black Swift is resident near Pafuri (Lanner Gorge) and a fairly common winter (June–August) visitor elsewhere in Kruger, while Common Swift is a regular spring and summer (October–March) visitor to the park. African Black Swift has a high-pitched screaming "*zzzzzzzzZZZZTTT*" call. Masters of the air, foraging birds can cover 1,000 km in a day, and often gather at termite emergences and fires to hawk insects.

☐ African Palm-Swift L: 18 cm (7")

A slim grey-brown swift with a long, deeply forked tail, often held closed in a single spike. The flight is distinctive, being weak and erratic, low over the tallest trees. This is a common resident throughout Kruger, nesting and roosting in *Borassus* and *Hyphaene* palms. They drink and feed on the wing, and use their tiny legs with hook-like claws to cling to the underside of palm fronds. The nest is stuck to a palm frond using the birds' glue-like saliva, and remarkably includes down feathers that have been dislodged from other birds in the air! For extra security, the eggs are also stuck to the nest.

☐ Little Swift L: 14 cm (5·5")

Small, compact and direct-flying, this dark swift has a distinctive square white rump patch and a square tail – all other 'white-rumped' swifts having longer, forked tails. The flight action consists of regular bouts of flapping and soaring on stiff wings. This is an abundant resident in Kruger, nesting on a variety of man-made structures including many bridges. It is gregarious, gathering in large numbers near roost sites at dawn and dusk, and issuing shrill chittering calls.

☐ White-rumped Swift L: 15 cm (6")

A small, dark, slender swift, with a narrow white crescent over the rump, and a forked tail with long, pointed sides. The flight action is elegant, fluid and effortless, with the tail often held closed forming a point. This is a common migrant (August–May) breeder to Kruger, with some birds overwintering. It is normally less common than Little Swift, and less gregarious, but will join mixed swift foraging flocks. The White-rumped Swift is an aggressive nest thief, often commandeering nests of swallows and Little Swifts by ejecting or smothering their chicks. It sometimes breeds co-operatively, with assistance from the previous year's offspring.

AFRICAN BLACK SWIFT

AFRICAN PALM-SWIFT

LITTLE SWIFT

WHITE-RUMPED SWIFT

Mosque Swallow L: 22–26 cm (9–10")

This large swallow has rusty-red underparts, a pale buff throat, and white underwing coverts that are obvious only in flight. It may be confused with juvenile Red-breasted Swallows, which have a pale throat, but that species always has dark ear patches and buffy underwing coverts. Although it is resident throughout Kruger, the Mosque Swallow is rare in the far south and fairly common only north of Shingwedzi, where its preferred breeding sites, cavities in large baobabs, become more frequent.

Barn Swallow L: 19 cm (7·5")

This common migrant swallow has long tail streamers, plain cream-white underparts, a broad dark collar, rusty-chestnut throat patch and white spots across the spread tail. Immatures are duller than adults and have shorter tail streamers. The Barn Swallow is an abundant non-breeding visitor (September–May) from Eurasia to all parts of Kruger. It is only likely to be confused with the Wire-tailed Swallow (*page 206*), which differs in having a white throat and an extensive chestnut cap. Its flight action is strong and fluid and large groups may gather to forage on aerial insects; it also forms large flocks in March and April before departing for the breeding grounds in the northern hemisphere.

Red-breasted Swallow L: 20–24 cm (8–9")

A large swallow with brick-red underparts and dark blue upperparts, told from other swallows by its metallic-blue 'drooping' ear patches. In flight its buffy underwing coverts differentiate it from the Mosque Swallow, which has white underwing coverts and a pale throat. The flight action is strong, with frequent swoops and changes of course. This is a common intra-African breeding migrant (August–March) in Kruger. It is most frequently encountered in the south of the park, becoming increasingly uncommon towards the far northern parts, where it is largely replaced by Mosque Swallow.

RED-BREASTED SWALLOW

RED-BREASTED SWALLOW

MOSQUE SWALLOW

BARN SWALLOW

MOSQUE SWALLOW

BARN SWALLOW

WIRE-TAILED SWALLOW

ROCK MARTIN

LESSER STRIPED-SWALLOW

☐ **Wire-tailed Swallow** L: 14 cm (5·5")

A small, delicate swallow with dark blue upperparts and plain white underparts, including the throat, and a neat chestnut cap extending from the bill to the nape. Adults have long, fine tail streamers, whereas these are lacking in immature birds, which are also browner. The flight action is weak and fluttering, often changing course. The much rarer White-throated Swallow (not illustrated) is similar but has a complete collar and the rust on the crown is restricted to the forehead. The Wire-tailed Swallow is a common resident throughout Kruger, where it is most often seen feeding over wetlands, and frequently nests under bridges, even during the winter months (June–August).

☐ **Lesser Striped-Swallow** L: 15–19 cm (6–7·5")

A distinctive burnt-orange skullcap extending onto the cheeks like a helmet, and boldly streaked underparts characterize this swallow. The similar but larger Greater Striped-Swallow (not illustrated) is much rarer in Kruger, and has fewer and finer streaks, especially on the throat and ears, giving it a more open-faced appearance. The Lesser Striped-Swallow has a strong flight action, much like that of Barn Swallow, and is a common intra-African breeding migrant (August–April) to Kruger, although some overwinter. It appears to favour man-made structures as breeding sites, which may have aided its spread into the region.

☐ **Rock Martin** L: 15 cm (6")

A dumpy-bodied, square-tailed dark brown swallow with a pale cinnamon throat and diagnostic white spots in the tail. This species is an uncommon and very local resident in Kruger, preferring rocky gorges and cliffs, where it breeds. It often joins other swallows and swifts when feeding, and may be attracted to bush fires. The flight is quite strong but fluttering, with frequent changes in course.

WIRE-TAILED SWALLOW

LESSER STRIPED-SWALLOW

ROCK MARTIN

Kruger is rich in nocturnal birds, supporting 11 owls and six nightjars. Some of these can be seen within camps; others are only likely to be encountered on official night drives, or with specific searching. Nightjars have small bills but wide gapes, rather flat heads, long wings, long, broad tails and tiny feet. They catch insects in the air, either in twisting flight or during brief sallies from the ground. Owls are familiar upright, large-headed nightbirds with large, forward-pointing eyes.

☐ Square-tailed Nightjar L: 24 cm (9")

This is the only nightjar in Kruger with a pale trailing edge to the wings and entirely pale outer tail feathers – white in the male and buff (in poor light can appear dark) in the female. At rest, it differs from the Fiery-necked Nightjar by having more white in the upperwing, and brown-grey (rather than chestnut) cheeks. It is a common resident throughout Kruger in wooded areas, although it is more patchily distributed in the north. The call is a long, monotonous, low, insect-like *"rrrrrrrrrrr"*.

☐ Fiery-necked Nightjar L: 24 cm (9")

This nightjar has pale corners to the tail – white in the male and buff in the female. It also has white patches in the wings, although these are less extensive than in Square-tailed Nightjar. At rest, it shows extensive chestnut on the cheeks (Square-tailed Nightjar has brown-grey cheeks), but the identification of perched nightjars can be difficult. This is the commonest resident (although some may migrate) nightjar in Kruger and is found in most types of woodland. Its loud, tremulous, whistling call *"Good Lord, deliver us"* is an evocative and frequent sound of the savannah at night.

FIERY-NECKED NIGHTJAR

SQUARE-TAILED NIGHTJAR

☐ **Barn Owl** L: 36 cm (14")

A medium-sized, ghostly pale owl with a distinctive heart-shaped face. It has creamy-buff underparts and golden upperparts flecked with silver-grey. This is a fairly common resident throughout Kruger, favouring open savannah, restcamps or areas with clearings, although numbers probably fluctuate depending on rodent abundance. Barn Owls fly slowly and buoyantly over open areas looking for prey, especially rodents. They have an extraordinary adaptation for hunting small mammals that have acute hearing: small serrations on the leading edge of the wing reduce turbulence and help them fly silently. The distinctive call is a piercing *"schreeeee"* scream that sounds demonic, and has inspired folk names such as 'death owl' or 'hobgoblin owl'. Despite being a successful predator, Barn Owls themselves often fall prey to larger owls.

▪ African Scops-Owl L: 17 cm (6·5")

This tiny, compact, camouflaged grey-brown owl has small ear tufts that form slightly rounded corners to the top of the head. It is a common resident throughout Kruger in a variety of woodlands. Most camps have a pair or two, which are most easily found either by speaking to camp staff who know the whereabouts of roosting birds, or by following their croaking or purring frog-like *"prreeeuup"* calls at night (occasionally also heard during the day). The calls are repeated every 5–8 seconds, sometimes for long periods. This owl's choice of natural cavities as nest sites often brings it into direct competition with hornbills, sometimes leading to the owls being killed.

☐ **Pearl-spotted Owlet** L: 19 cm (7·5")

This small, rounded, brown-and-white owl is often active during the day. It has white speckles over its back and tail, and diagnostic white spots (not bars) on the fore-crown and head. White-ringed black markings on the back of the head give the impression of false eyes. The similar but rarer African Barred Owlet (not illustrated) is larger, has bars (not spots) on the head, and lacks 'false eyes'. The Pearl-spotted Owlet is a common resident in wooded savannah throughout Kruger, including many camps. It gives an accelerating series of high-pitched, upslurred, piping *"fwooo"* notes followed by a set of downslurred *"puuueeeww"* whistles, and can often be heard and seen by day, when it may attract a mob of small birds that will antagonise it until it flies away on whirring wings with an undulating flight like a woodpecker. This owl is a hole-nester that prefers abandoned barbet and woodpecker holes and, like the African Scops-Owl, competes with starlings, rollers, hoopoes and hornbills for nesting cavities.

☐ **Verreaux's Eagle-Owl** L: 60–66 cm (24–26")

An enormous greyish owl with dark stripes framing the face, a silver-grey bill and large, dark eyes with strange and diagnostic fleshy-pink eyelids. Although this is a widespread resident throughout Kruger, it occurs at low densities, preferring areas with large riverine trees for roosting, but avoiding forest. This is the largest owl in Southern Africa, and the most fearsome winged nocturnal predator in Kruger. No medium-sized nocturnal mammal is safe, with hares, genets and mongooses frequently being taken as prey, as are sleeping monkeys and roosting francolins and guineafowl. Reptiles, insects and other invertebrates also form part of its varied diet. The call is a deep, grunting *"unngh-unngh"*. Verreaux's Eagle-Owl often clashes with the almost-as-large Pel's Fishing-Owl (*page 214*), the latter frequently coming off second best.

☐ **Spotted Eagle-Owl** L: 43–47 cm (17–19")

A large, grey-brown owl with obvious ear tufts and bright yellow eyes – a combination of features that is unique among Kruger's owls. This resident owl is common and widespread in many habitat types in the park, and can often be seen on night drives. It feeds on a wide variety of prey that is mostly hunted from a perch. The typical call is a soft, booming *"whooo-whooo"* or *"whoo-are-you"*.

One of the BIG 6

EN ☐ Pel's Fishing-Owl L: 51–63 cm (20–25")

'Old Ginger' is probably the most near-mythical of all the bird species in Kruger. It is an unmistakable giant, oval, ginger-rufous owl adorned with black bars and chevrons. It has large and piercing deep, dark eyes, and 'puffy' feathers on the neck and head that give it a rounded profile. This bird is so seldom seen that it would not normally feature in a book of this nature, but its status as one of Kruger's flagship 'Big 6' birds, its striking appearance, amazing behaviour, and much-desired status amongst birders earn it inclusion. A small population of 30–40 pairs is estimated to occur along Kruger's rivers, with most on the Olifants (6–10 pairs), Sabie (2 pairs) and Limpopo and Levuvu (12–15 pairs) Rivers. The Levuvu and Pafuri region in particular offers the best chance at finding one in Kruger, especially if you can arrange a walk with a ranger. However, it could appear along any major river, especially in times of drought, so keep your eyes peeled. The call is a deep, horn-like *"boom"* and a series of grunts. Young sometimes emit an eerie screeching *"wheeeuuu"* call. Erosion and increased river turbidity, caused by modifications to upstream river catchments, are growing threats to this iconic species. Pel's Fishing-Owls are quite shy, whevener possible avoiding skirmishes with Verreaux's Eagle-Owls (*page 212*) and African Fish-Eagles (*page 189*) that sometimes try to occupy their territories. It roosts, well hidden, in huge trees along permanent rivers that hold sluggish backwaters where it hunts after dark for fish, particularly catfish and pike, and sometimes amphibians. These owls are perfectly adapted for fishing, having spiky scales on unfeathered legs that enables them to grasp slippery catfish. Unlike most owls, it hunts mainly by sight, and since hearing and silent flight are unimportant, its hearing is not particularly acute and it lacks noise-reduction edgings to the feathers, making it a noisy flyer. The fish can't hear them coming anyway!

Further reading

This book focusses on the birds you are most likely to encounter during a safari in Kruger. Inevitably, with over 500 species recorded in the park, you may come across a bird that is not covered and want to know what it is. You may also want to know more about the other animals you encounter on your travels. If this is the case, do not despair – there are a number of books that cover all of the birds recorded in South Africa, and a sister guide to this publication that covers the mammals, reptiles and frogs you are likely to see. These are listed below as recommended further reading.

Barnes, K. *Animals of Kruger National Park*. Published in 2016 in the Princeton **WILD***Guides* Wildlife Explorer series by Princeton University Press.

Carnaby, T. *Beat about the bush* – birds. Published in 2008 by Jacana Media

Chittenden, H. and Whyte, I. *Roberts Bird Guide Kruger National Park and adjacent lowveld*. Published in 2009 by the John Voelcker Bird Book Fund.

Fourie, P.F. *Kruger National Park Questions and Answers*. Published in 2014 by Struik.

Hilton-Barber, B and Arthur, L. *The Prime Origins Guide to Best Birding in Kruger*. Published in 2008 by Prime Origins.

Hockey, P.A.R., Dean, R. and Ryan, P.G.R. *Robert's Birds of Southern Africa*. Published in 2005 by the John Voelcker Bird Book Fund.

Sinclair, I., Hockey, P., Tarboton, W. and Ryan, P. *SASOL Birds of Southern Africa*. Published in 2011 by Struik.

Tarboton, W. and Ryan, P. *Guide to Birds of the Kruger National Park*. Published in 2016 by Struik.

Taylor, M.R., Peacock, F. and Wanless, R.M. *The 2015 Eskom Red Data Book of Birds of South Africa, Lesotho and Swaziland*. Published in 2015 by BirdLife South Africa.

Online resources

www.adu.org.za – The amazing animal demography unit runs a variety of bird-based citizen science projects, from atlassing to road counts. Anyone can get involved so if you have a yearning to contribute to some citizen science, check out what is on offer.

www.sanparks.org – South African National Parks website and booking portal. Extensive information relating to the park, and also the way to book your own stay.

www.krugerpark.co.za – Your one-stop shop for private and self-drive safaris and loads of information regarding the park.

www.facebook.com/groups/krugerparkearth/ – Largest and most active Facebook community sharing photos, information and stories about Kruger Park.

Acknowledgements

Mark Lorenz commented on the manuscript. Iain Campbell and Richard Barnes each joined Keith in the field for a week and also contributed their images. Keith's parents, wife and son all had their holidays turned into chances to take photos for the book, and their understanding is appreciated. Thanks to the many photographers whose photos appear on these pages, and to the Tropical Birding clients with whom we have had the privilege of sharing the magnificence of Kruger. The team at **WILD**Guides – Rob and Rachel Still, Andy and Gill Swash, and Rob Hume – thanks so much for helping make sure the content was there, the details accurate and for designing a beautiful book. Robert Kirk at Princeton, thanks for believing in this project.

Photographic credits

All the images included in this book were taken by the authors, apart from the following:

Christian Boix: Pel's Fishing-Owl (*p. 215*). **Iain Campbell:** Spur-winged Goose on ground (*p. 32*), Ruff (*p. 51*), Curlew Sandpiper (*p. 51*), Pied Kingfisher female (*p. 52*), Black-crowned Tchagra (*p. 133*), White-crested Helmet-Shrike (*p. 137*), Village Indigobird female-type (*p. 162*), Wahlberg's Eagle main image (*p. 186*), Black-shouldered Kite hovering (*p. 200*), African Scops-Owl main image (*p. 210*). **Roger and Liz Charlwood** (WorldWildlifeImages.com): Yellow-billed Egret in flight (*p. 22*), Eurasian Hobby perched (*p. 194*). **Greg and Yvonne Dean** (WorldWildlifeImages.com): Yellow-billed Egret on ground (*p. 22*), African Finfoot male and female (*p. 41*), Grey-headed Kingfisher (*p. 95*), European Bee-eater (both) (*p. 96*), Southern Masked-Weaver male (*p. 151*), African Dusky Flycatcher (*p. 174*), Mosque Swallow on ground (*p. 205*). **Erni** (Shutterstock): Little Grebe juvenile (*p. 33*), Common Sandpiper (*p. 47*), Red-backed Shrike male (*p. 77*). **Richard Flack**: Red-headed Weaver female (*p. 152*). **Philip Fourle** (flickr.com/photos/philipf): Collared Sunbird male (*p. 146*), White-bellied Sunbird male (*p. 147*). **Johann Grobelaar:** Greater Honeyguide male (*p. 111*). **Lizet Grobelaar:** Lesser Honeyguide (*p. 110*), Greater Honeyguide female (*p. 111*), Orange-breasted Bush-Shrike (*p. 134*), White-winged Widow breeding male (*p. 154*), Amur Falcon perched (both) (*p. 195*), Fiery-necked Nightjar (*p. 208*), Square-tailed Nightjar (*p. 208*). **Marc Guyt** (Agami.nl): Laughing Dove (*p. 83*), Common Scimitarbill (*p. 103*). **Hugh Harrop** (shetlandwildlife.co.uk): Red-backed Shrike female (*p. 77*), Willow Warbler (*p. 127*). **Charley Hesse:** Red-faced Cisticola (*p. 56*). **Chris Krog:** Purple-crested Turaco (*title page*), Barn Owl (*p. 13*), Brown-hooded Kingfisher (*p. 95*). Broad-billed Roller perched (*p. 99*), Violet-backed Starling male (*p. 138*), Thick-billed Weaver female (*p. 149*), Red-collared Widow male (*p. 155*). **Sheau Torng Lim:** Southern Boubou (*p. 176*). **Leon Marais:** Double-banded Sandgrouse (inset) (*p. 71*), Klaas's Cuckoo male (*p. 90*), Bennett's Woodpecker (both) (*p. 113*), African Goshawk (*p. 196*), Gabar Goshawk dark (*p. 198*). **Karel Mauer** (Agami.nl): Common Ostrich male (*p. 58*), Hadeda Ibis in flight (*p. 59*). **David Monticelli** (Agami.nl): Namaqua Dove male (*p. 83*). **Dave Montreuil** (flickr.com/photos/davemontreuil): Collared Sunbird female (*p. 146*). **Daniele Occhiato** (Agami.nl): Grey Heron (*p. 20*), Little Egret in flight (*p. 22*), Lesser Grey Shrike (*p. 77*), Steppe Eagle (*pp. 178 & 187*). **Ran Schols** (Agami.nl): Amur Falcon (*p. 195*). **Hira Punjabi** (Alamy Stock Photo): Wire-tailed Swallow (*p. 206*). **Benji Schwartz:** Grey-headed Bush-Shrike (*p. 135*). **Dave Smallshire:** African Green-Pigeon perched (*p. 167*). **Walter Soestbergen** (Agami.nl): Malachite Kingfisher (*p. 52*). **Andrew Spencer:** Chestnut-backed Sparrowlark male (*p. 72*). **Philip Stapelberg:** Grey Tit-Flycatcher (*p. 131*). **Andy and Gill Swash** (WorldWildlifeImages.com): Yellow-billed Stork in flight (*p. 27*), Hamerkop in flight (below) (*p. 29*). African Sacred Ibis on ground (*p. 29*), Little Grebe non-breeding (*p. 33*), Common Moorhen (*p. 39*), African Jacana in flight (*p. 40*), Water Thick-knee on gound (*p. 42*), Blacksmith Lapwing (*p. 45*), Three-banded Plover (*p. 47*), Wood Sandpiper (*p. 47*), Marsh Sandpiper (*p. 48*), Ruff in flight (both) (*p. 50*), Cattle Egret on ground (*p. 59*), Abdim's Stork on ground (*p. 61*), Marabou Stork on ground (*p. 62*), White Stork (both) (*p. 63*), Crowned Lapwing (*p. 69*), African Stonechat (both) (*p. 75*), Red-eyed Dove (*p. 85*), Jacobin Cuckoo (*p. 88*), Diederik Cuckoo female (*p. 90*), European Roller in flight (*p. 100*), European Roller (*p. 101*), Dark-capped Bulbul (*p. 119*), Yellow-billed Oxpecker juvenile (*p. 142*), Red-billed Oxpecker juvenile (*p. 143*), Scarlet-chested Sunbird female (*p. 145*), Lesser Masked-Weaver male (*p. 150*), Red-billed Quelea female (*p. 153*), Red-billed Firefinch male and juvenile (*p. 157*), Cut-throat Finch female (*p. 159*), Long-tailed Paradise-Whydah male (*p. 161*), African Paradise-Flycatcher female (*p. 175*), White-backed Vulture (both) (*p. 177*), Brown Snake-eagle (*p. 179*), Black-breasted Snake-eagle immature (*p. 179*), Hooded Vulture (both) (*p. 181*), White-backed Vulture (both) (*p. 183*), Tawny Eagle (*p. 187*), African Hawk-Eagle (both) (*p. 190*), Bateleur perched (both) (*p. 191*), Eurasian Hobby in flight (*p. 195*), Dark Chanting-Goshawk main image (*p. 199*), Black Kite in flight (from above) (*p. 201*), African Harrier-Hawk main image (*p. 201*), Barn Swallow in flight (*p. 205*), Rock Martin (*p. 207*), Verreaux's Eagle-Owl (*p. 212*). **Warwick Tarboton** (warwicktarboton.co.za): Black Heron (*p. 25*). **Markus Varesvuo** (facebook.com/markus.varesvuo): Little Egret (*p. 23*), Namaqua Dove in flight (both) (*p. 82*), Namaqua Dove female (*p. 83*). **Scott Watson:** African Crowned Eagle (*p. 192*). **Brendon White** (flickr.com/photos/bwildlife): Rock Kestrel (*p. 197*).

In addition, the following images are reproduced under the terms of the Creative Commons Attribution-ShareAlike 2.0 UK: England & Wales License or the Attribution-ShareAlike 4.0 International License:

Scientific names of the bird species included in this book

Most of the guides working in Kruger, and the majority of visitors, use English names when referring to the birds they see. However, some species have more than one English name, and given the diversity of countries from which visitors to the region come, these names may not be familiar to all. To help those visitors who know the birds by their universally accepted scientific name, the following list has been prepared. This includes all the birds mentioned in the book, ordered alphabetically by their scientific name. It is cross-referenced to the English name(s) used and the page number(s) on which the bird appears. English names are highlighted in **bold** for those species that are illustrated, and for ease of reference the page number for the main account for each of these species is shown in **bold**; other places in the book where a photograph appears are indicated in *italics*. The other species mentioned in the book that are not illustrated are shown in normal text.

Index

Names in **bold** highlight those species that are afforded a full account. Alternative names by which the species is known are given in brown text for ease of reference. **Bold** numbers indicate the main species account. *Italicized* figures relate to other page(s) on which a photograph appears. Normal black text and numbers are used for species that are not illustrated. For scientific names, see *page 218*.

223